Essential Psychology
for Medical Practice

STUDENT NOTES

Essential Psychology for Medical Practice

Andrew Mathews PhD

Professor of Psychology,
St George's Hospital Medical School,
University of London

Andrew Steptoe DPhil

Reader in Psychology,
St George's Hospital Medical School,
University of London

CHURCHILL LIVINGSTONE
EDINBURGH LONDON MELBOURNE AND NEW YORK 1988

CHURCHILL LIVINGSTONE
Medical Division of Longman Group UK Limited

Distributed in the United States of America by
Churchill Livingstone Inc., 1560 Broadway, New
York, N.Y. 10036, and by associated companies,
branches and representatives throughout the world.

First published 1988

ISBN 0-443-03423-0

British Library Cataloguing in Publication Data
Mathews, Andrew M.
  Essential psychology for medical practice
  1. Psychology. 2. Medicine and psychology
  I. Title. II. Steptoe, Andrew
  150'.2461   BF131

Library of Congress Cataloging in Publication Data
Mathews, Andrew M.
  Essential psychology for medical practice/Andrew Mathews, Andrew
  Steptoe.
      p.   cm.
  Bibliography: p.
  Includes index.
  1. Psychology. 2. Medicine and psychology. I. Title.
  [DNLM: 1. Psychology. 2. Psychosomatic Medicine. 3. Physician
-Patient Relations. BF 121 M429e]
  BF121.M4   1988
  150—dc19

Produced by Longman Singapore Publishers (Pte) Ltd.
Printed in Singapore

Preface

This book has gradually evolved from its origin as a set of lecture notes used in the behavioural science course at St George's Hospital Medical School, London University. While many textbooks of psychology were already available, we continued to feel the need for a single concise source that would convey the essentials of psychological knowledge required for medical practice. We have thus tried to combine two aims: to demonstrate the basis of psychology in experimental research and objective measurement of behaviour; and to show that the resulting knowledge has considerable relevance to medicine. Indeed, we believe that behavioural science has at least as much direct relevance to medical practice, in all its varied forms, as do some other disciplines which are taught in greater detail to medical students, but find relatively little application thereafter. At the same time, we feel that it is important to avoid allowing our own interest and enthusiasm for the science of psychology to burden the reader with lengthy discussions of issues mainly of interest to other psychologists. We have therefore attempted to discard any material which does not have both medical relevance, and a sufficient basis in empirical research, to justify its inclusion.

For these reasons, we think that this book should be particularly suited to the needs of both pre-clinical and clinical medical students, and to those qualified medical and health professionals who feel the lack of information about progress in psychological science. In general, the chapters progress from the more basic biologically oriented topics in psychology, to more complex psycho-social issues, such as doctor/patient communication. Thus we begin by considering the ways in which the brain processes and stores environmental information, and what may go wrong with these functions. In subsequent chapters, we consider how behaviour is modified as the result of experience, the development of ability through the life span, personality differences, and the nature of emotion. The remaining chapters are more directly organised around medical issues; behavioural causes of disease, the problem of pain, emotional disorders and their treatment, communication with patients, adherence to treatment, and the promotion of health. Throughout the book we have tried to make explicit the applications of psychological research by inserting highlighted sections which describe clinical examples, case descriptions or other relevant medical material. To help provide more background on the actual findings and methods of psychological research, we have listed sources for further reading after each chapter, together with study questions to guide readers in assessing their comprehension of what has been covered.

Like other sciences, psychology is an evolving body of knowledge and ideas, and perhaps the most important omission from this book is that of direct involvement with the excitement and uncertainties of research progress. Many of the 'facts' of today are the discarded theories of tomorrow, whether in physics, physiology, or psychology. Despite these uncertainties, we hope that readers will find enough in the pages which follow to interest them in keeping abreast of future research developments, in what has yet to become 'essential psychology for medical practice'.

Department of Psychology,   A. M.
St George's Hospital Medical School   A. S.

Acknowledgements

We should like to thank Margaret Reuben and Sue Arnold for their efficient and willing secretarial assistance. Our thanks also to the students over several years at St George's Hospital Medical School, whose responses to our teaching have helped to shape this book.

Acknowledgements

Contents

1

Psychological functions and the brain

Psychological functions such as behaviour, thought and emotion depend on the action of the brain. Very few psychological processes are sustained by single regions of the brain without simultaneously involving other areas. Nevertheless, some basic distinctions can be made between the operations performed in different brain regions, since there is considerable specialisation of function at both the cortical and subcortical levels. Three fundamental functional areas can be identified, and these are illustrated in Figure 1.1.

(a) *The brain stem and hindbrain.* These are responsible for the maintenance of arousal and neural tone, the regulation of many peripheral physiological processes, and the control of the sleep–waking cycle. These processes are discussed in Chapter 2.

(b) *Subcortical structures.* Subcortical structures such as the hypothalamus, basal ganglia and limbic system can be incorporated into a second functional unit. They are involved with the regulation of emotional behaviour, and the integration of behaviour with autonomic and neuroendocrine output. The psychological significance of these structures is discussed in Chapters 2 and 6.

(c) *The cerebral cortex.* The neocortex underpins many complex psychological functions, and lesions in this area may lead to deficits in higher cognitive processes such as language, memory and thought. However, the cerebral cortex is not autonomous or independent of subcortical structures, and it may not even be the highest level of integration for some operations such as motor control.

Several techniques have been developed for investigating brain function. They include: *electrical or chemical stimulation*, either at the surface of the cortex, or with implanted electrodes; *electrophysiological recording* from the surface of the brain to produce the electro-encephalogram (EEG), or with single-cell recordings from fine electrodes lowered into deeper layers; *measures of local metabolic activity*, by means of radioactively labelled tracers that index

1

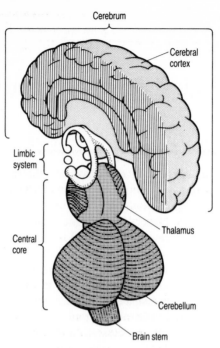

Fig. 1.1 Exploded view of the human brain. The brain stem, hindbrain and limbic system are shown in their entirety, but the left cerebral hemisphere has been removed.

glucose uptake or regional blood flow in the brain. *Mechanical, chemical and electrical lesions* are studied in both animals and humans. Investigations in humans have traditionally relied on studying patients with neurological damage. Subtle cognitive and behavioural tests have been devised that tap specific deficits and abilities. There are, however, a number of problems in the interpretation of deficits resulting from brain damage.

Inferences from brain lesions

The nature and history of the lesion may affect the deficits that are observed. Brain damage may be acute, as in the case of traffic accidents, or slow and insidious. With slow onset, the patient may have been living with the dysfunction for several years, and may have learned to cope with it. Lesions also vary in their localisation, from the precise tissue damage resulting from gunshot and war wounds to the diffuse necrosis following a cerebral stroke. The lack of precise anatomical information about the extent of tissue damage often makes interpretation of functional deficits difficult. Experimental lesions in animals are more precise, but changes in performance tests must be interpreted carefully, since even simple tasks involve a number of different processes (perceptual discrimination, motivation, attention, memory, motor response execution and so on). The same apparent performance deficit may follow disturbances in any one of these functions.

The age at which brain damage occurs is also crucial. The brain has remarkable powers of plasticity and recovery of function. Even areas of brain tissue that are thought to have unique and specialised properties (such as those underlying language) are not irreplacable, provided that damage occurs early in life.

CORTICAL LOCALISATION OF FUNCTION

The survival and safety of human beings and animals depend on the regulation of behaviour by external and internal information. There is a continuous interplay between sensory input and action or behaviour as the organism responds to needs and changing circumstances. However, not all events registered by the sensory receptors are consciously perceived or stored.

Information processing refers to the sequential activity of the brain through which sense data are received, selected, analysed, interpreted and stored. Figure 1.2 outlines the regions of the cerebral cortex that are of major functional significance. A useful distinction can be made between activities in the anterior and posterior portions of the neocortex divided by the central sulcus or fissure. The posterior (caudal) portion (including the occipital, parietal and temporal lobes) is largely concerned with the perception, analysis and storage of information. Particular areas are specialised for the reception of information in each sense modality, while adjacent zones perform higher analyses of these inputs. The anterior portion is concerned with motor output and the planning and execution of programmes of behaviour.

Neuropsychology of perception

Information entering the sense organs undergoes a series of complex transformations beginning at the receptor level onwards. After initial processing in which significant features such as contours or changes in stimulus strength are extracted at the

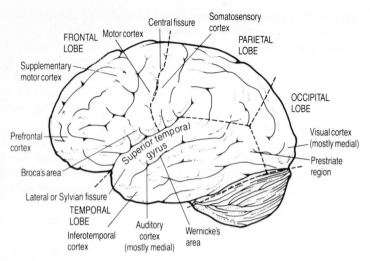

Fig. 1.2 Lateral view of the left cerebral hemisphere.

expense of less valuable information, central integration synthesises these elements into a meaningful whole (*perception*).

Single-cell recording

The studies of Nobel Prize winners Hubel and Wiesel using single-cell recording techniques have extended our understanding of how this process is carried out in the visual system. The pattern is summarised in Figure 1.3. Each neurone in the system is responsive to illumination in a particular part of the visual field. The *receptive fields* of neurones change their properties and size from retina to the cerebral cortex. At the earliest stage, there are various types of retinal ganglion cells, each of which has a central receptive field surrounded by an inhibitory zone (or vice versa). Since receptive fields overlap extensively, combinations of these 'on/off' cells provide information on the localisation of illumination within the visual fields. The projection of the visual pathways through the lateral geniculate nuclei to the cortex is systematically ordered, so that adjacent parts of the visual field are represented close to each other in the occipital or visual cortex (topographic projection).

Within the visual cortex, a number of different response characteristics and cell types are found. *Simple cells* (found mainly in lamina IV) respond optimally to lines, edges or slits in a particular orientation within the receptive field. A slight rotation in the

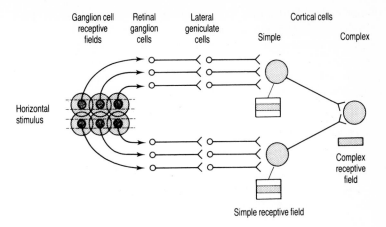

Fig. 1.3 Hierarchical model connecting cells involved in visual perception, showing the feature extraction that takes place at different levels. (From Levitt 1981)

stimulus may abolish the cell response. *Complex cells* have larger receptive fields, and respond to stimuli of a specific orientation, moving in a certain direction. *Hypercomplex cells* are responsive to the length of the stimulus as well as its orientation and direction of movement. They can therefore detect corners as well as edges. Outside the primary visual cortex, cells have been found in pre-striate and inferotemporal regions that respond to more complex stimuli. Response to colour, contrast, position and even specific patterns have been recorded. Most cortical cells respond to stimulation of either eye.

Perceptual processing

These investigations have led to the *trigger feature hypothesis* of visual perception outlined in Figure 1.3. At each level cells receive both excitatory and inhibitory inputs from units at more peripheral levels. The interplay between these signals means that increasingly precise information is extracted as inputs are transmitted through the systems.

Beyond these early stages of simple feature processing, little is known at the neurological level. It is assumed that further processing occurs in which stimulus elements are integrated to allow the perception of meaningful shapes. However, other evidence shows that the visual processing system is biased in favour of perceiving forms that can be interpreted in the light of past experience. Perception is not simply a passive mechanism for extracting information from the environment, but an active process in which hypotheses are generated by the brain on the basis of partial information. These hypotheses are then tested by comparison with sensory input.

Perceptual learning

Early experience influences the development of these perceptual processes. Kittens exposed only to vertical (or horizontal) stripes for the first months of life subsequently show deficits that result from an inability to respond to other contours or orientations. It is possible that cortical cells are 'uncommitted' at birth, and become sensitive to particular stimuli with experience. This experience must be acquired during a critical period early in life.

Perceptual learning in adults has been studied by asking volunteers to wear prismatic lenses that alter the retinal image (eg, invert it). After a period of confusion, subjects adapt to the new visual input and regain their perceptual skills. When the lenses are removed, the same difficulties are found in reverse. These experiments indicate that the interpretation of sense data is not fixed, but is modified by learning.

Higher processing of special senses

Information in each sensory modality is projected to a different primary reception area in the cortex (see Fig. 1.2). The auditory cortex lies on the superior temporal gyrus, while information concerning touch and kinesthesis is projected to the somatosensory cortex. Anatomical and behavioural studies indicate that the information extracted in the primary reception area is projected transcortically to the adjacent *association cortex* for further processing. Lesions in these association areas may lead to deficits in learning and memory tasks dependent on the interpretation of percepts rather than simple loss of sensation. Integration of material processed in separate modalities takes place in the posterior region of the neocortex.

Abnormalities of perception

Perceptual abnormalities may arise from damage of the cerebral cortex, depending on the area and level of processing disrupted. For example, lesions of the primary visual cortex result in simple visual field defects. Damage to the inferotemporal cortex on the other hand may result in an inability to recognise objects (visual agnosia). Lesions in the parietal lobe can lead to deficits in tactile perception, body sense and spatial orientation. They may be associated with spatial neglect (in which patients fail to pay attention to an area of space or their own bodies) and apraxia, or loss of intentional movement.

Motor processes

The motor cortex is the area immediately anterior to the central sulcus. Studies in which the surface of the motor cortex is stimulated indicate that the various parts of the body are represented in the motor cortex, as is illustrated by the motor 'homunculus' in Figure 1.4. The amount of cortex dedicated to each portion of the

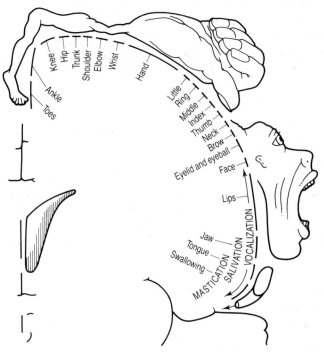

Fig. 1.4 The motor homunculus, showing proportional representation in the motor cortex.

body depends on the sophistication of movements required; consequently, the hands, face and speech mechanisms have the largest representation.

The motor cortex is not the only brain region concerned with movement. Other cortical regions such as the frontal supplementary motor region are also involved, while subcortical regions (basal ganglia and cerebellum) are implicated in the integration of both voluntary and involuntary movements. The proximity of the motor and somatosensory cortex suggests they are closely integrated in regulating fine movement.

Prefrontal cortex

The prefrontal cortex has no direct involvement in the processing of sensory information, and its functions are poorly understood. Phylogenetically, the prefrontal cortex is the most recently developed region of the brain, and comprises about a third (by mass) of the cerebral hemispheres. It receives transcortical inputs from the temporal, parietal and occipital lobes, and is richly interconnected with the limbic system. Studies of regional blood flow indicate that frontal activity predominates when a person is in a resting state, undisturbed by sensory stimulation or motor activity. It has been suggested that the frontal lobes have an executive role, planning and co-ordinating motor acts and skills.

Prefrontal damage

Patients with lesions in the prefrontal area show disturbances in intentional behaviour and in the flexibility of response patterns. They fail to adapt to changing circumstances, and do not correct errors of performance. Difficulties with problem solving are therefore common. Sometimes striking alterations in social behaviour are observed, with euphoria, impulsiveness, a loss of social inhibitions and a lack of concern for the future.

HEMISPHERE DIFFERENCES

The two cerebral hemispheres receive *contralateral* inputs from sensory systems. Afferents from the right ear, right visual hemifield and right side of the body project to the left hemisphere, while motor pathways from the left hemisphere regulate the right arm and leg (and vice versa). The two hemispheres are connected by the cerebral commisures. Processes regulated in the two hemispheres are not identical, since there is functional specialisation or *lateralisation* of some activities.

Lateralisation of language

Language is the most important lateralised function. Deficits of speech, comprehension and written language regularly occur with damage to the left hemisphere. In contrast, many people show no language disturbances following right hemisphere lesions. It might be expected that this lateralisation of language function is related to handedness — language being located in the hemisphere that controls the hand used for writing. However, the majority of left-handed people also have speech representation in the left hemisphere.

A clear way of determining speech representation in the brain is the Wada test, in which sodium amytal is injected into one carotid artery. This temporarily depresses the hemisphere supplied by that artery, and thus provides information about speech representation. Results from a large series are presented in Table 1.1. Studies of this kind demonstrate that more than 95% of right-handed people have speech representation in the left hemisphere. The proportion is lower in left-handed and ambidexterous people; although some 70% still have left hemisphere speech some of the left-handed and ambidexterous subjects show bilateral speech representation. However, the brain shows considerable plasticity in this respect. Many people who sustain left cerebral damage early in life go on to develop adequate speech sustained by the right hemisphere. This effect is more marked among left-handed or ambidexterous subjects. Thus although language is normally later-

Table 1.1 Speech representation in patients of different handedness on the Wada test

| | *n* | Speech representation (%) | | |
		Left	Bilateral	Right
Without early left-sided damage				
Right handers	140	96	0	4
Left/mixed handers	122	70	15	15
With early left-sided damage				
Right handers	31	81	6	13
Left/mixed handers	78	30	19	51

From Rasmussen & Milner 1975.

alised in the left hemisphere, the right hemisphere may take over when necessary. There appears to be a developmental sequence, in which lateralisation of speech progresses gradually as the brain matures. The extent of speech recovery following damage to the left hemisphere is inversely related to age.

Right hemisphere function

Although the left hemisphere is primarily responsible for language functions, some related abilities are also shown by the right hemisphere. After loss of the left hemisphere in adults, residual functions such as automatic speech (recitation of the alphabet, etc.), singing and emotive speech may remain. In contrast, certain deficits are characteristic of damage to the non-speech hemisphere. Spatial disorientation is common, with disturbances in recognition and judgement of spatial relationships. This suggests that the right hemisphere has specialisations of non-verbal functions.

Cerebral commissurotomy

One method of investigating the functions of the two cerebral hemispheres is to sever the cerebral commissures, so that the two half-brains function independently. Extensive studies have been carried out on patients who have undergone cerebral commissurotomy for the alleviation of severe epilepsy (*split-brain* patients). Considering that over 200 million fibres connecting the two hemispheres are cut, it is striking that patients continue to function successfully after the operation. Deficits only emerge when information is presented to one hemisphere only.

The basic pattern results from the fact that only the left hemisphere has access to sophisticated speech mechanisms. If a light is presented in the right visual field (projected to the left hemisphere), the patient will report seeing it as normal. The patient will deny seeing a light in the left visual field, but can nevertheless point to the stimulus with the left hand. Objects handled by the left hand cannot be named, but can be matched non-verbally to visual targets.

The right hemisphere has some limited ability to comprehend language. For example, if a simple word is flashed to the left visual field, this can be matched to objects (although it cannot be spoken). The right hemisphere is superior on spatial tasks such as face recognition, block designs and tactual recognition of complex patterns.

Brain and mind

Studies of split-brain patients have been used to demonstrate that mental life is dependent on the action of the brain. Split-brain patients have two distinct, independent realms of consciousness, each with its own memories, skills and endowments. In effect, they have two minds, each corresponding to the functions performed by one of the two hemispheres. The mind is not independent, supervising brain functions in a disembodied fashion. This is illustrated in the following account by a woman who has undergone cerebral commissurotomy for the management of severe epilepsy. Remember that only the left hemisphere can talk, and that the left hand is directed by the right hemisphere.

'My left hand is under control, but yet it grabs things that it shouldn't grab, or it grabs things I don't want it to grab. It just sort of reaches out, like that. I don't like the idea of that, because I don't know what is happening. Sometimes I just take my right hand and grab hold of my left hand or arm and pull it back. Other times, it may sound silly, but I slap it because I get mad at it, I really do, I get really mad at it, and I find that doesn't do any good, except it hurts after it's slapped.' (From Gilling & Brightwell 1982)

Lateralisation in the normal brain

We are not normally aware that the two cerebral hemispheres are specialised for different functions, or that our efficiency at task performance depends on how the information is presented. This is because information is generally projected bilaterally, and there is rapid transfer between the hemispheres through the commissures. However, specialisation of the hemispheres can be studied with dichotic listening tests. Different messages are sent simultaneously to the left and right ears. When subjects are later asked to recall or recognise what they heard, one or other ear may have the advantage, according to the type of material presented. Verbal material presented to the right ear is recognised more accurately than that presented to the left. The reverse is true for melodies. The same pattern has been shown for visual inputs: when images are flashed to the visual half-fields, normal subjects recognise faces, complex stimuli and inverted numbers faster with the right hemisphere. These differences are extremely small, presumably because inputs to the 'wrong' hemisphere are rapidly transferred through the commissures.

Nature of hemisphere differences

Table 1.2 summarises the functions that are lateralised in the brain. There is disagreement about the underlying nature of these differences. It has been suggested that the specialisations concern not only language, but a fundamental dichotomy in cognitive processing. The left (verbal) hemisphere is associated with analytical and reductive processes, while the right employs synthetic, holistic methods. Whatever the difference, the brain normally operates with continual rapid transmission between the hemispheres, and the overall output is integrated.

Table 1.2 Summary of lateralised processes

Function	Left hemisphere	Right hemisphere
Visual system	Letters, words	Complex geometric patterns; facial recognition
Auditory system	Language-related sounds	Non-language environmental sounds; music
Somatosensory system		Tactual recognition of complex patterns; Braille
Movement	Complex voluntary movement	
Memory	Verbal memory	Visual memory
Language	Speech; reading; writing; arithmetic	
Spatial processes		Geometry; sense of direction; mental rotation of shapes

LANGUAGE AND THE BRAIN

The traditional view that the left hemisphere is dominant because it sustains language and intelligent functions has been replaced by an interactive model of *complementary specialisation* of function.

Higher functions such as intellectual ability emerge as integrated programmes of behaviour, and depend on the dynamic interactions of brain regions.

Cortical speech areas

The relationship between language and the brain has largely been inferred from language disorders following strokes and other brain lesions. Two areas of the left hemisphere appear particularly important, and they are associated with different types of speech deficit. These regions are illustrated in Figure 1.2. The area lying in the third frontal gyrus was identified as significant in speech by Paul Broca in 1861; it is now known as *Broca's area*. Broca's area lies near the region of the motor cortex responsible for facial movements, and the aphasia seems to be linked with motor or expressive defects.

The second important area for speech lies in the posterior portion of the superior temporal gyrus. It is known as the posterior speech zone or *Wernicke's area*. Comprehension may be impaired, while speech lacks meaning. Studies of patients with brain damage suggest that speech disorders occur with many other lesions, for example when the arcuate fasciculus, interconnecting Wernicke's and Broca's regions, is cut. Disorders of naming (anomia), reading and writing are more common when the angular gyrus is damaged.

Speech disorders following brain lesions

Damage to Broca's area results in non-fluent speech. Speech is laboured, inarticulate and ungrammatical, often with a 'telegraphic' style in which unimportant words are omitted. However, meaning is transmitted effectively, and comprehension is good. Patients with lesions in Broca's area seem to have access to the lexicon or vocabulary, but have lost syntax. For example, when asked what he did during the week, one Broca's patient replied 'Monday . . . Wednesday . . . speech . . . therapy'. The meaning was clearly transmitted, even though few words were used.

In contrast, patients with Wernicke's aphasia speak fluently and articulate well. However, speech lacks content and appears to be vague and irrelevant. Words may be invented or used inappropriately, and there may be comprehension deficits. An example of Wernicke's aphasia is this response to a request to describe a picture:

'Dahnay. Enambalsay. Fack-anadee. Whynownea. Oldeea. Eggerferma gerfriend.' Examiner: 'What's he doing?' Patient: 'Goin' tagowi. She's got a rablium. I think I wanta . . . Oh he . . .' Examiner: 'Do you know what this is over here?' Patient: 'No. Balky. I-isetinga.' (From Beaumont 1983)

FURTHER READING

Beaumont J G 1983 Introduction to neuropsychology. Blackwell, Oxford
Luria A R 1973 The working brain. Penguin, London
Springer S P, Deutsch G 1985 Left brain, right brain (2nd edn). W H Freeman, Oxford

STUDY QUESTIONS

1. What is the evidence for cortical localisation of function?
2. What methods can be used to study the functions of the brain?
3. What have single-cell recordings taught us about perceptual processes?
4. What is meant by lateralisation of function in the brain?
5. How has the study of split-brain patients thrown light on normal cerebral function?
6. Outline the deficits associated with damage to the frontal (Broca) speech zones.

2

Sleep, arousal and motivation

The intensity of behavioural activity varies along a dimension of arousal that encompasses both wakefulness and sleep, as can be seen in Figure 2.1. Arousal is rather a vague term and can be defined in many different ways, from level of alertness and behavioural performance efficiency to autonomic and physiological activation. Brain activity itself can be monitored with EEG recordings, where increasing levels of alertness are generally reflected in low amplitude, high frequency patterns. In contrast, alpha waves (8–12 Hz) dominate the EEG of the resting awake person. This chapter describes the psychological importance of the arousal dimension, beginning with sleep.

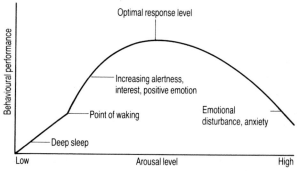

Fig. 2.1 The effects of level of arousal on behavioural performance.

PATTERNS OF SLEEP

Sleep is characterised by physical inactivity together with a loss of awareness and responsivity. EEG recordings have shown that sleep is not a unitary state, but that systematic variations in brain activity occur. Sleep has been categorised into a number of stages, shown in Figure 2.2.

15

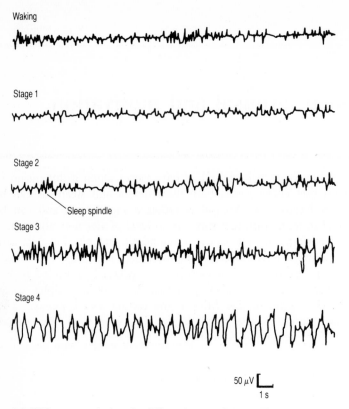

Waking

Stage 1

Stage 2

Sleep spindle

Stage 3

Stage 4

50 μV

1 s

Fig. 2.2 EEG patterns during the different stages of sleep. (From Levitt 1981)

Stage 1 is the lightest sleep stage, and the first to be entered on falling asleep. The EEG shows a mixed frequency, low voltage pattern, with peaks of activity in the alpha and theta (4–7 Hz) wavebands;

Stage 2 consists primarily of theta activity, interrupted by sleep spindles (12–14 Hz) and high amplitude 'K' complexes;

Stages 3 and 4 are characterised by high amplitude, low frequency (2 Hz) delta waves. When these comprise more than 50% of the record, the subject is considered to have entered stage 4. Stages 3 and 4 are sometimes described as 'slow wave' sleep (SWS) or 'synchronised' sleep. Progression from stages 1 to 4 is marked by an increase in low frequency EEG activity at the expense of the higher frequencies typical of the waking state. At the same time, the sleeper becomes more difficult to arouse.

Rapid eye movement sleep

The pattern of sleep stages is complicated by the existence of rapid eye movement (REM) sleep, also known as 'desynchronised' or 'paradoxical' sleep. The EEG indicates cortical activation, with a mixed frequency low voltage pattern similar to waking or stage 1 sleep. This is associated with conjugate rapid eye movements, autonomic arousal (increased oxygen consumption, brain temperature and heart rate), penile erection and vaginal vasocongestion, together with a paradoxically low muscle tone. Despite the alert EEG, the individual is hard to rouse, but when sleepers are woken from REM sleep they frequently report dreams.

Sleep cycles during the night

The sleep stages recur in a cyclical pattern during the night, and this is illustrated in Figure 2.3. An initial progression through stages 1 to 4 is followed by regular oscillation between REM and non-REM stages. REM phases are repeated at approximately 90-minute intervals, and add up to some 20% of total sleep time. Slow wave sleep is concentrated in the early part of the night, while REM sleep episodes become progressively longer with each sleep cycle.

This pattern is typical of the healthy young adult, but there are enormous variations between individuals in total sleep time and

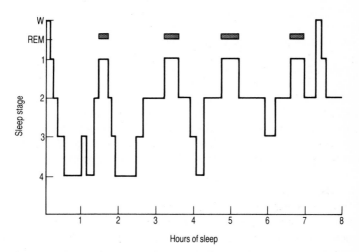

Fig. 2.3 Typical pattern of sleep stages in a healthy young adult.

sleep stages. Some people can do with very little sleep, and can survive happily with less than 3 hours of sleep a night. Changes also occur with age. The proportion of total sleep time spent in REM is high in neonates (up to 50%), but falls rapidly over the first few years of life. Sleep in the night often becomes shorter in the elderly, but may be compensated by a greater incidence of daytime naps. However, the elderly are also more frequently disturbed in the night, and this may lead to complaints of sleeplessness and prescription of drugs to help sleep.

Insomnia

Insomnia is a complaint about the inadequate quantity or quality of sleep, and usually concerns difficulty in going to sleep, frequent awakenings during the night, or early morning arousal. The problem is not simply related to length of sleep, since total sleep time in people complaining of insomnia often differs little from average. Additionally, the reported disturbance of sleep (such as total sleep time and latency before falling asleep) tends to be greater than that measured objectively with EEG recording. Many poor sleepers exaggerate sleep disturbances, and do not find themselves refreshed by sleep. Poor sleep may be caused by a number of problems, including psychiatric disturbance (particularly depression), stimulating drugs (including caffeine), respiratory impairment and nocturnal myoclonus (restless legs syndrome). Another common cause is the use of hypnotic drugs (ironically prescribed for sleep problems), since these interfere with REM activity and may produce excessive REM and rebound insomnia when drugs are withdrawn. Surveys indicate that up to one-third of people are unhappy about the quality of their sleep, with more frequent complaints among women.

Psychological methods can be valuable in managing sleep problems, and relaxation techniques are often recommended. Another approach is to modify the environment associated with sleep (stimulus control), so that the bedroom and its contents become cues for sleep rather than activity. Hence, poor sleepers are discouraged from reading, eating and watching television in bed, since these activities are incompatible with sleep.

FUNCTIONS OF SLEEP

Sleep is necessary for survival, and sleep deprivation generates intense desire for sleep. Nevertheless, the function of sleep and its various stages has not been established. The fact that dreams are associated with REM sleep, and that this form of sleep is also highly prevalent in infancy, has led to the theory that REM sleep is important for psychological function. Slow wave sleep on the other hand is a period of physiological quiescence in which metabolic restoration might take place. This view is supported by the observation that growth hormone is secreted during SWS. However, these distinctions are only partially supported by sleep deprivation studies.

Sleep deprivation

Sleep deprivation studies may involve restriction of total sleep time, or selective deprivation of SWS and REM. Early investigations of REM deprivation showed dramatic emotional reactions, supporting the involvement of the stage in psychological processes. But more systematic investigations have failed to show specific cognitive impairments with REM sleep deprivation that do not occur with deprivation of other types of sleep.

Selective deprivation of sleep stages results in rebound effects following the experimental period. Over the next few nights, more time is spent in the stages which were deprived, suggesting that the person needs to catch up with lost types of sleep. It is not clear why this is the case. However, following total sleep deprivation, it is interesting that more SWS than REM sleep is recovered. Individuals who naturally sleep very little also show high levels of SWS. It seems that human beings are more able to dispense with REM than with SWS.

Dreams

When people are woken from the different stages of sleep, dreams are described in about 80% of awakenings from REM sleep, and only 20% from non-REM sleep. It has been argued that the eye movements characteristic of REM are related to dream content, but the evidence is inconsistent. From the psychoanalytical point of view, dreams reflect subconscious mental processes that are repressed during normal consciousness. Other views have related dreams to information processing and the incorporation of recent experience into memory. Experiences of the recent past are frequently relived in dreams, albeit in unexpected forms. However, none of these theories are easy to test systematically, and the possible distortion of dream content during the recall process must be taken into account when assessing the function of dreams.

Sleep disruption and health

Sleep loss has important effects on behavioural performance efficiency, and may lead to deterioration in a variety of information-processing tasks. In addition, sleep disturbance may have adverse health consequences. A number of studies have shown that various types of shift work lead to disruption of sleep behaviour and eating habits, and an increase in symptoms (particularly digestive disorders and gastrointestinal complaints). It is not clear whether these result from disruption of *circadian rhythm* or loss of sleep. Individuals vary considerably in their adaptability to shift and night work, and selection of people suitable for such occupations may be beneficial.

MECHANISMS OF SLEEP AND ACTIVATION

Early theorists assumed that sleep was a passive process resulting from reductions in brain activity following diminished sensory input. However, brain lesion studies by Bremer and others have demonstrated that sleep is an active process governed by brain stem mechanisms. Figure 2.4 summarises the effects of brain stem transection at different levels, as assessed by EEG patterns and measurement of pupil responses. A state of somnolence follows the *cerveau isolé* (midcollicular lesion), which separates the cerebral hemispheres from the midbrain. On the other hand, a regular sleep–waking cycle is maintained with the *encéphale isolé*, in which the brain is isolated from the spinal cord. The third 'midpontine' lesion leads to a state of wakefulness, despite the lack of sensory inputs.

These studies imply two distinct functional regions: a lower brain stem sleep-promoting area, and a higher arousal area. Injection of the barbiturate sedative thiopental into arteries serving the upper arousal area puts an animal to sleep, while wakefulness follows administration of the drug to the sleep-promoting area. The arousal mechanism has been linked by Moruzzi & Magoun with the ascending reticular activating system (RAS).

Reticular activating system

This is a diffuse multisynaptic network of neurones projecting

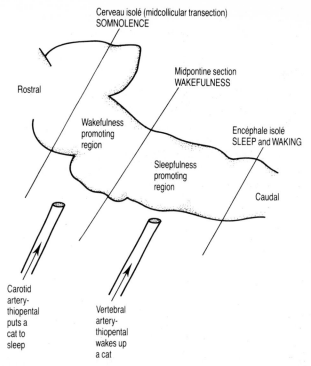

Fig. 2.4 An outline of the effects of three brain stem transections and thiopental injections on sleep and wakefulness. (From Levitt 1981)

through the brain stem and thalamus to higher brain centres (see Fig. 2.5). Stimulation of the RAS elicits an activated EEG in the cortex while arousing behavioural, autonomic and neuroendocrine mechanisms. It has a crucial role in modulating the general level of behavioural alertness and efficiency.

The RAS has intrinsic activity, but also receives collateral inputs from ascending somatosensory pathways. Thus stimuli that impinge on the individual are not only projected by specific sensory pathways, but contribute to the general level of arousal. This pattern has led to the activation theory of RAS function, in which the network has a generalised non-specific arousing role in the nervous system, and a reciprocal relationship with behaviour. The RAS enables the organism to respond appropriately to external stimuli, while behaviours in turn are executed in order to restore the equilibrium of arousal. Conditions of extreme sensory stimulation and consequent high levels of arousal will therefore be

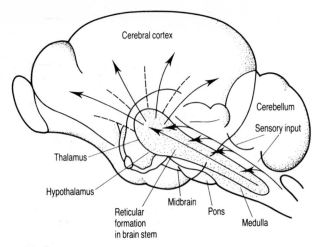

Fig. 2.5 The projection of the ascending reticular activating system to the cerebral cortex.

avoided. Activation theory has been criticised on the grounds that activation and arousal are not unitary phenomena, since different indices of arousal (behavioural, subjective, autonomic and EEG) are poorly correlated. Nevertheless, the theory is in keeping with the disruptive effects of excessive sensory stimulation and arousal on behaviour. Low levels of stimulation are also disturbing, as can be seen in *sensory deprivation* studies. In these experiments, volunteers are isolated in soundproof rooms, with their limbs wrapped in padding and opaque goggles over their eyes. Such conditions rapidly produce disturbances in thought, concentration and behavioural performance, together with visual and auditory hallucinations.

Arousal and performance

The relationship between arousal and behavioural performance has been outlined in Figure 2.1. Performance improves from low to intermediate levels of arousal, but then deteriorates. This inverted 'U' or curvilinear relationship has been documented for a variety of tasks. For example, you may drive a car perfectly well when practising, but the additional arousal produced by a driving test may lead to mistakes and a loss of skill. For every task there is an optimal level of arousal, and this is lower for more difficult tasks. Thus a simple task will be performed more accurately and efficiently at a relatively high level of arousal, while a lower level is required for a hard task.

Performance efficiency for a variety of tasks fluctuates over the day in a pattern that is related to the diurnal rhythm of physiological activation. Efficiency in carrying out simple tasks such as visual searching increases over the day with a peak in the early evening, paralleling the rise in body temperature. However, other tasks such as those using short term memory (see Chapter 3) actually show deterioration over the day.

MOTIVATION

Motivated behaviours are actions directed towards fulfilling some goal or need, or the avoidance of unpleasant conditions. Basic motives such as hunger, thirst, the avoidance of pain and protection of the young are called *primary drives*. Many primary drives arise from physiological need states, and serve to motivate behaviours that restore or maintain the homeostatic balance. Other behaviours are not motivated directly by primary needs, but may develop through processes of conditioning and learning (see Chapter 3).

DRIVE AND THE BRAIN — *hunger*

Eating is a good example of the way in which motivated behaviour is organised and represented in the brain. The hunger drive leads not only to eating, but to working for food; thus a rat in an experimental apparatus may press a lever many times in order to receive a food pellet. However, not all eating is homeostatic, as we know from common experience. Our eating behaviour is influenced by sensory factors (taste, palatability, etc.), and we may eat appetising foods even when we are satiated. Some animals also prefer saccharine to neutral-flavoured substances, even though saccharine has no nutritive value.

The regions of the brain associated with hunger have been investigated with stimulation and lesion techniques. The key area is the hypothalamus, different regions of which have opposing functions, as is shown in Figure 2.6. Stimulation of the ventromedial nucleus (VMN) of the hypothalamus will reduce eating even in a hungry animal , while destruction of the VMN leads to overeating. The reverse effects are seen with the lateral hypothalamus (LH), where lesions lead to loss of eating behaviour (aphagia). This has led to

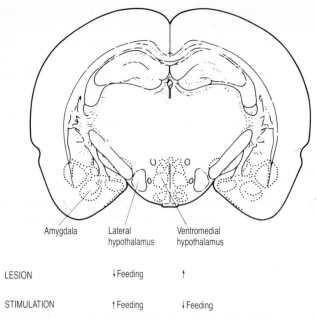

Fig. 2.6 Transverse section of the rat brain at the hypothalamic level, showing the effects of lesions and stimulation. (Reprinted with permission from Rolls (1975), Pergamon Books Ltd.)

the notion that the LH is a 'feeding' centre, while the VMN is a 'satiety' centre. After lesions of the satiety centre the feeding centre will operate unchecked, leading to overeating.

However, the full picture is more complicated. Animals with lesions to the VMN show a hypersensitivity to taste, and only gain weight when fed with palatable food. They do not show high drive levels, since they will not work for food. On the other hand, animals with LH lesions eventually recover from their aphagia and begin to regulate weight once more. It may be more appropriate therefore to consider the hypothalamic nuclei as regions concerned with processing sensory (LH) and nutritive (VMN) information related to eating. Thus, following VMN lesions, eating is governed by sensory factors, while lesions to the LH lead to a loss of interest in food. Single-cell recordings from the lateral hypothamalus have shown diminution of responding when an animal has eaten a particular food to satiety, though the cells responded once more when a new flavour was presented, suggesting sensory-specific effects in the hypothalamus. It should also be remembered that many other organs and mechanisms, including the gastrointestinal tract, the liver and the autonomic nervous system, are concerned with the regulation of food intake.

Eating disorders

The most important psychological eating disorder is anorexia nervosa, in which eating is reduced to very low levels, leading to extreme weight loss and sometimes death through self-starvation. Anorexia is most common in adolescent girls and young women, and has been linked with cultural pressures (society's admiration for extremely slender figures) and psychological conflicts (fear of growing up and sexual maturity). Anorexia often appears to take the form of a phobia of becoming fat, even in extremely emaciated victims. A related problem is bulimia nervosa, in which extreme dieting is interspersed with periods of bingeing and vomiting.

It is not certain whether obesity should be considered an eating disorder since, contrary to popular beliefs, scientific studies have shown that obese people do not generally eat any more than average. Metabolic disorders may be more important, with disturbances in the heat regulation mechanisms that normally dispose of unwanted calories. However, it has been found in some experiments that obese people are more sensitive than others to food palatability. They may also eat under conditions in which other people do not eat, for example when depressed or anxious. Emotions may thus have become cues for eating in an uncontrolled way.

Electrical self-stimulation

Direct evidence concerning the brain mechanisms of drive and motivation has emerged through studies of electrical self-stimulation of the brain (ESB). This was discovered by James Olds, who found that when electrodes were implanted in certain brain regions, animals found stimulation rewarding. In a typical experiment, a rat receives brief stimulation every time it presses a bar. Extraordinarily high rates of ESB occur, with animals persisting without rest for many hours, even neglecting to eat and drink. ESB seems to be equivalent to natural rewards. For example, food deprivation increases the amount of self-stimulation in the LH, while ESB is reduced in the satiated animal. Other manipulations that affect the hunger drive also influence ESB. In Figure 2.7, it can be seen that the hypoglycaemia produced by insulin injection increases ESB,

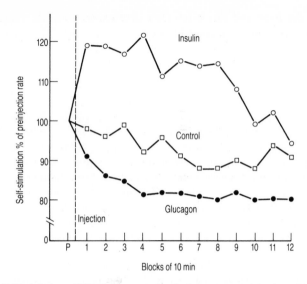

Fig. 2.7 Modulation of ESB by hunger signal. Subcutaneous injection of insulin increases lateral hypothalamic self-stimulation, while glugagon has the opposite effect. (Reprinted with permission from Balagura & Hoebel (1967), Pergamon Books Ltd.)

while stimulation rates are reduced following the hyperglycaemia produced with glucagon.

Brain regions and electrical self-stimulation

The regions where stimulation is rewarding include many nuclei in the hypothalamus, the medial forebrain bundle and other subcortical sites. This suggests that the hypothalamus may be part of a larger reward system, and that this system is accessed directly by ESB. Catecholamine neurotransmitter pathways may mediate these effects. Drugs affecting brain catecholamines lead to changes in ESB; for instance chlorpromazine blocks ESB, while apomorphine (which stimulates dopamine receptors) leads to increases in ESB. In contrast, stimulation of some other sites, including the medial hypothalamus and periventricular zones, is aversive or punishing. The two systems interact, since stimulation in reward sites can counteract the effects of stimulating punishment pathways. ESB is seldom elicited from neocortical sites.

Electrical self-stimulation has been observed in many species including primates. A few studies have been carried out with people into whom electrodes have been implanted for medical reasons. Although stimulation appears to be very rewarding, the reports of what it feels like are unfortunately vague.

SEX DRIVE

Sex drive results from an interaction of physiological and hormonal predispositions with external stimuli and learning history. Circulating hormones are crucial in sexual differentiation and determine not only the development of male and female genitalia, but changes at sexual maturity and the periodic fluctuations of fertility and sexual activity in adult animals. The hypothalamic nuclei involved with sexual function develop from a common neural substrate, and differentiate under the influence of circulating androgens. These nuclei are concerned both with cyclical hormonal activity and with sexual behaviour itself.

The study of sex drive is complicated by the fact that there is a much weaker link between sexual behaviour and hormonal state in humans than in other animals. For example, castration of mature male rats leads to decreases in sexual behaviour that can be restored by injection of testosterone. Castration has a smaller effect on men, while among non-castrated males the amount of sexual activity correlates poorly with hormone levels. A similar pattern is seen among females. Ovariectomised animals lose all concern and interest in sexual behaviour, while many women find their sex drive is unaffected by ovariectomy.

On the other hand, the experiential or learning component of sexual behaviour is more important in humans than lower animals. Rats reared in isolation are able to copulate when mature, provided that appropriate sensory stimuli are present. The same is not true of monkeys, which show severe disturbances of sexual behaviour if raised in isolation. In humans, the expression of sex drive is predominantly learned. This is reflected in the wide variety of sexual behaviours that are found, and in the cultural definition of sexual attractiveness (see Chapter 5).

FURTHER READING

Boddy J 1978 Brain systems and psychological concepts. John Wiley, Chichester
Levitt R A 1981 Physiological psychology. Holt, Rinehart and Winston, New York
Rolls E T 1975 The brain and reward. Pergamon Press, Oxford

STUDY QUESTIONS

1. What is the normal pattern of sleep in adults?
2. Outline the brain mechanisms modulating arousal.
3. How can the functions of sleep be investigated?
4. Describe the neural substrate for motivated behaviour.
5. What is the relationship between electrical self-stimulation and natural reward?
6. Does human sexual behaviour depend on hormonal state?

3

Memory and learning

Learning and memory are often used in conversation to mean the same thing; but in psychology they are defined differently. Memory refers to the processes whereby information is retained by the nervous system, and includes the initial *acquisition*, *storage* and subsequent *retrieval* of that information. Learning, on the other hand, is usually defined as a relatively permanent change in behaviour resulting from experience. It is clear that any such change must depend on information being stored in the nervous system, but information is sometimes stored without resulting in behaviour change. Learning is thus a more restricted concept than memory, although an emphasis on observable behaviour has led to a number of useful practical applications that will be considered later. In the first half of this chapter we will consider the more general topic of memory, subdivided according to the stages of acquisition, storage and retrieval.

MEMORY

Acquisition and selective attention

The acquisition of information from the environment depends on the allocation of processing resources to that information, and we refer to the voluntary allocation of resources as *selective attention*. The central nervous system cannot register and store all the information entering the sensory receptors; important data must be selected while the rest is ignored. For example, we can attend to a far-off conversation while ignoring another that is nearby. Information ignored in this way does not appear to be stored, since it cannot be recalled later. However, there is evidence that such unattended information is processed to a limited extent, although it may never become conscious.

This unconscious processing can be studied using the so-called '*dichotic listening*' technique in which one of two different messages is presented to each ear. Attention is directed to one channel by asking the subject to repeat aloud what they hear in that ear (shadowing). Although material from the unattended channel is not normally heard consciously, highly meaningful words (such as the subject's own name) may break through and be detected. This could not happen if the unattended channel was not being continuously processed.

Similar partial processing without awareness may also occur during sleep. Things said to a patient when unconscious during surgery cannot be consciously recalled, but are more easily relearned than new material which had not been presented in this way. Despite such evidence of unconscious learning, it is apparent that learning proceeds much more efficiently when attention is focused on the task in hand, so that patients with poor attention control tend to find new learning difficult or impossible.

Attention and mental illness

Brain damage or psychosis is often associated with failure in selective attention. In schizophrenia, for example, patients may find it difficult to avoid paying attention to irrelevant or meaningless stimuli around them, and so become confused or disorientated. One schizophrenic patient described his experience in the following way:

Everything seems to grip my attention although I am not particularly interested in anything. I'm speaking to you just now but I can hear noises going on next door and in the corridor. I find it difficult to shut these out and it makes it difficult for me to concentrate on what I am saying to you. (From McGhie & Chapman 1961)

Sensory registers

Each sensory system appears to have a very brief holding store, from which attended information is passed for further processing. Input from retinal images is held briefly in a visual register which decays rapidly over a few seconds. A very brief (50 milliseconds) visual display can still be read for up to a second or so after it has in fact disappeared. The rate at which this visual register appears to decay depends on subsequent input, so that fading is slowed by a period of darkness following stimulation. Similar rapidly decaying stores have been demonstrated in other sensory systems such as hearing.

Short Term Memory (STM)

If a new combination of familiar material is learned, such as a telephone number, it appears to be held in a short term store that has a longer decay time than do sensory registers. Furthermore, decay can be prevented by voluntary rehearsal, such as mental repetition of the new telephone number. If rehearsal is prevented by requiring another task to be performed, forgetting of a new number or letter string is virtually complete after about 20 seconds. There is a definite limit to the amount of information that can be stored in STM — about seven items (plus or minus two) in people of normal intelligence. The number of items an individual can hold (*memory span*) is fairly constant.

Short term memory is involved in conscious decision making or problem-solving operations such as mental arithmetic. Hence, the ability to solve problems is progressively reduced as one is required to hold increasing amounts of other information in STM. Although the neurophysiological processes involved are ill understood, STM probably depends on the pattern of electrical activity in neuronal networks, since it is sensitive to the effect of electroconvulsive shock (ECS) to the brain. Memory span following limited brain damage (e.g. to the temporal lobes) is usually normal, although recall over longer periods may be grossly deficient. This implies that information can get into the system, but that the long term storage and/or retrieval process has broken down.

Long Term Memory (LTM)

What we normally think of as 'memory', that is, a record of past events and the representation of meaning, appears to have different properties than does STM. The capacity of long term memory is too large to be measured at present, and is certainly greater than that which can be consciously recalled. Direct stimulation of the temporal cortex in conscious patients undergoing brain surgery often elicits reports of vivid but previously unrecalled events from the past. The patient's conviction that the recalled events are real, whether valid or not, suggests that the temporal lobes are involved in the retrieval process. Some patients with damage to the temporal lobes or nearby limbic structures can remember long past events, but not those that have occurred since the damage took place.

Normally, long term memories are encoded to allow associative links with information having similar meaning. For example, if

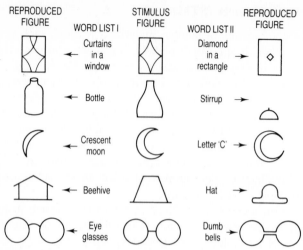

Fig. 3.1 Effect of labelling on the perception and reproduction of figures. The central figure was the stimulus and the outside ones were examples of reproduction (from Carmichael et al 1932, copyright APA. Reprinted by permission of the author).

ambiguous pictures are given particular verbal labels, later reproduction of the pictures is systematically distorted to fit better with the labels given to them (Fig. 3.1). Although these distortions provide evidence that associative meaning is used to code information, sensory-specific stores are also thought to exist in LTM. The use of visual imagery when learning verbal material is known to result in exceptionally good long term recall, suggesting that multiple encoding using both visual and semantic memory systems enhances retrieval.

Long term memory appears to depend on permanent changes in neurone structure, since protein synthesis inhibitors injected into the brain prevent the formation of long term memories, but do not interfere with already established memories.

One memory or several?

Evidence for separate memory systems can be summarised as follows:
1. Decay rates vary from rapid to extremely slow, depending on whether memories are new or well established.
2. Error patterns reveal that different types of encoding occur over time, with abstract (less sensory-specific) meaning predominating in the longer term.

3. Brain damage can affect long term recall of new information, but not short term recall (or vice versa).

This does not necessarily mean that memory consists of totally separate stores; but rather that it involves a series of stages in processing and storing information. These stages are illustrated in Figure 3.2.

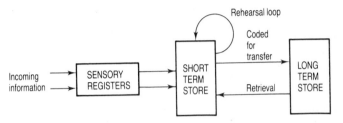

Fig. 3.2 Diagram of typical model of stages in storing information. Sense data is held briefly in sensory registers, some being selected for transfer to STM (or possibly directly to LTM). Information can be maintained in STM by rehearsal, and may be coded for transfer to LTM or lost (forgotten). Information that reaches LTM may be available for retrieval into STM (adapted from Atkinson & Shiffrin 1971).

This diagram should not be taken literally; rather, it summarises the most common view about processing stages that was held by memory researchers at that time. We already know that it is incomplete in several respects: for example, rehearsal is only one of the ways in which items may be passed to LTM, and it is clear that information may be stored in LTM without passing through STM at all, and without our being aware of the process. Evidence for this comes from experiments on very briefly presented words, in which subjects can guess the general meaning of words quite accurately even at presentation times too fast for them to identify any physical properties of the word, or even to be sure that a word was present at all. Furthermore, it is now thought that STM (referred to as working memory) may be subdivided into a central executive, an articulatory loop (used for rehearsal) and a visuo-spatial holding store.

FORGETTING

After new material has been learned the amount that can be recalled decreases rapidly at first, and then more slowly until the residual retained after a few days shows little further loss. The amount of loss is much greater if a second set of new material follows shortly after the first, indicating that forgetting depends on interference between competing memories rather than simple decay. If a large amount of material is presented (such as a long list of words) and then immediately recalled, items presented either first or last are better remembered than those in the middle. After a delay, the advantage for material presented last disappears (as information is lost from STM), leaving the material presented first as best recalled. A final factor that determines forgetting is the nature of the material itself; meaningful information (that can be encoded in terms of existing knowledge) is much more likely to be retained.

Helping patients not to forget advice

When patients leaving a consultation have been asked to recall what they were told by their doctor, they have been found to forget up to half of the information they were given. Memory for medical advice (as opposed to diagnostic information) can be particularly poor, especially in the case of highly anxious or elderly patients (see Table 3.1). General or abstract statements (such as 'you need to watch your weight') are more difficult to remember than are more specific concrete suggestions (such as

Table 3.1 Summary of data showing effects on the probability of remembering statements: (a) according to type or position of statement; (b) with or without explicit categorisation of statements; (c) before or after use of memory aid rules by doctor (adapted from Ley 1977)

(a) *Percentage recalled by patients according to type and position of information*:

General statements	16
Specific statements	51
Importance of statements stressed	69
Statements given first	87

(b) *Percentage recalled of different types of information according to whether categorised or not*:

	Usual	Categorised
Diagnostic	61	67
Advice	28	65
Other	46	70

(c) *Percentage recalled by type of patient according to whether memory aid rules were used by doctors*:

	Before	After
Children	62	73
Adult	58	70
Elderly	42	64

'you need to weigh yourself every day'). Statements made early on in a series seem more likely to enter LTM (the *primacy effect*). Statements made at the end of a consultation are remembered better initially but then tend to be forgotten. Statements in the middle of a list tend not to be remembered at all. Finally, information is assimilated better when it can be encoded in terms of meaningful categories, as shown by clinical studies in which items are grouped under simple headings (e.g. 'I will tell you: what is wrong . . ., what treatment you need . . ., what you can do to help yourself . . .'). Patients' recall can thus be maximised by using the following rules:

1. Provide the most important information (e.g. advice) early in any set of instructions.
2. Stress importance of relevant items (e.g. by repetition).
3. Use explicit categorisation under simple headings such as those described above.
4. Make advice specific, detailed and concrete rather than general and abstract.

THE AMNESIC SYNDROME

Different types of memory loss may follow concussion (traumatic amnesia) or more permanent brain injury, such as that associated with alcohol abuse or senile dementia.

Traumatic amnesia

Traumatic amnesia is characterised by loss of memory for events that occurred prior to the trauma (*retrograde amnesia*). It may initially cover several years, but gradually shrinks to a comparatively short time. The older memories usually return first, while the period immediately preceding the trauma may be permanently lost. There may be some post-traumatic amnesia as well, although this is commonly of short duration.

Traumatic amnesia can be illustrated by the effects of ECS, which has similar effects to an epileptic seizure. ECS immediately following new learning in animals abolishes the memory of that learning experience, but with increasing delays between learning and ECS the amount lost is progressively less. This might suggest that the lengthening interval permits transfer of the trace from a vulnerable electrical form into long term memory, where it is less susceptible to electrical scrambling. Experimental evidence, however, suggests that ECS does not prevent storage of new information in LTM, but rather blocks its retrieval (see following sections).

Organic amnesia

Following many types of brain damage, a memory deficit is seen for events that follow the damage (*anterograde amnesia*). Patients may be unable to learn any new material, although speech and personal memories from the past usually remain intact. STM is also intact (i.e the patient shows normal memory span, and thus can converse without difficulty). More rarely a deficit is apparent in STM with or sometimes even without problems in LTM. The existence of one type of memory deficit without the other provides additional evidence that these two aspects of memory depend on different processes.

Retrieval failure in amnesia

The failure of amnesic patients to learn new material, despite retaining previously established memories, can be explained in two ways. The failure may be one of transferring and fixing new material in long term memory. Alternatively it may be that material is successfully stored but then lost due to interference or some other forgetting process, so that it cannot be retrieved when it is required. The second theory is supported by the fact that accurate recall may be improved when amnesics are given cues or prompts consisting of fragments of the correct answer. An example of progressive improvement in cued recall is shown in Figure 3.3.

Retrieval failure may also account for some of the effects of traumatic amnesia. Memories that have been lost following ECS can sometimes be recovered by the use of prompts, or reminders. Conversely, previously established learning can be disrupted if it is being rehearsed at the time ECS is given. ECS therefore appears to disrupt the process of retrieval, rather than to obliterate memories completely.

LOCATION OF MEMORIES IN THE BRAIN

Complex memories are not easily removed by lesions of particular parts of the cerebral cortex. Hence, if animals have been taught a complex new behaviour, the extent to which that behaviour is lost

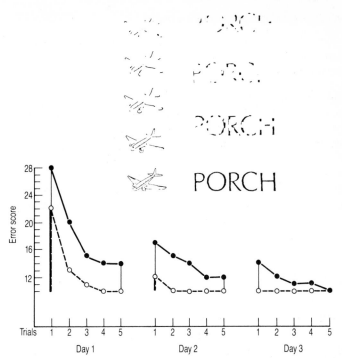

Fig. 3.3 Results of an experiment showing the effect of cued recall in amnesics. Subjects were presented with fragmented words or pictures of the type illustrated here, starting with the most fragmented forms. Ability to recognise the stimuli at a high level of fragmentation indicates that subjects are retrieving information stored in memory. The lower section of the figure shows the improvement in performance in amnesic subjects (solid lines) and normal controls (dotted lines). Note that performance improves over trials in amnesics, and that there is also retention across days (From Warrington & Weiskrantz 1968. Reprinted by permission from Nature, Vol. 217 pp. 972–973. Copyright © 1968 Macmillan Magazines Limited.)

depends on the total amount of cortical tissue removed, rather than the removal of tissue from any particular site. One explanation is that learned behaviours are multiply represented, so that removal of one type of representation leaves others intact. Memories of events are thus stored simultaneously in many regions of the cortex, although certain areas are particularly important in their retrieval. For example, damage to the dominant temporal lobe interferes somewhat with verbal recall; damage to the non-dominant lobe has a similar effect on non-verbal recall. Damage to both lobes, particularly if it involves the hippocampus, has a more profound effect, as is described below.

Types of damage leading to amnesia

Korsakoff's syndrome is an amnesic condition resulting from a vitamin deficiency associated with alcoholism. It leads to bilateral damage in the limbic regions, and in particular to the mamillary bodies and their connections with the hippocampus. Similar memory defects are found following viral encephalitis where damage to the hippocampal area results. Surgical lesions in the same area (provided that they are bilateral) also produce retrieval failure from LTM. Such clinical cases indicate that the medial temporal zone, and in particular the hippocampus, is involved in the laying down or retrieval of memory traces, but is not the actual site of storage. The function is evidentially bilaterally represented, since lesions to one side of the brain have a relatively small effect.

LEARNING

Behaviour of organisms low in the phylogenetic scale is dominated by innately determined responses, while the behaviour of higher organisms (such as humans) is greatly modified by learning. Although basic drives such as the need for food and social contact appear to be innate, their mode of expression is learned. For example, if young monkeys are reared in total isolation they react with fear to later contact with others, and are unable to form normal social and sexual relationships. Although much of human learning is symbolic (e.g. depends on thought and language), many of our more basic behaviours or emotional reactions are acquired through simple forms of learning such as conditioning.

CONDITIONING

Treatment of nocturnal enuresis

The treatment of nocturnal enuresis by the 'bell and pad' method illustrates some of the principles established in the laboratory study of learning. The enuretic child sleeps on two wire-gauze pads, separated by sheets, and connected to an electronic alarm. Wetting the bed triggers the alarm, waking the child and stopping further urination. Over a series of trials nocturnal urination becomes progressively less until it ceases, or the child wakes before urination begins. To understand how such treatment works it is necessary to consider the principles involved in classical and operant conditioning.

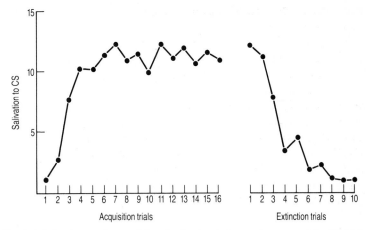

Fig. 3.4 Salivation to the conditioned stimulus (prior to the onset of the UCS) is plotted on the ordinate, and the number of trials on the abscissa. The CR gradually increases over trials and levels off at about 11–12 drops of saliva. After 16 acquisition trials the UCS is omitted, and the conditioned salivation is gradually extinguished.

Classical (or Pavlovian) conditioning

In Pavlov's early experiments, dogs were presented with food immediately following a signal that originally produced no reaction. After several pairings of the signal with food, the signal alone came to elicit progressively more salivation, up to an asymptote (see Fig. 3.4). The previously neutral signal is known as a *conditioned stimulus* (CS), as opposed to the food which in this case is the *unconditioned stimulus* (UCS). Salivation in response to the CS is referred to as the *conditioned response* (CR), and closely resembles the original response to food (the *unconditioned response* or UCR), although the CR and UCR often differ in subtle ways. If the CS is repeatedly presented without being paired with the UCS, then the CR gradually disappears, a process known as *extinction*.

Subsequent experiments have shown that almost any bodily response may be conditioned in this way. For example, if a person is repeatedly subjected to a puff of air to the eye or cold water immersion, following a particular signal, then that signal alone (the CS) will come to elicit eye blink or vasoconstriction (the CRs) that were previously produced only by the air puff or cold water. Signals that are similar, but not identical, to the original CS will produce weaker versions of the CR (*generalisation*). For example, an asthmatic patient who has experienced repeated attacks associated with the presence of a cat may then have episodes of wheezing triggered by a toy cat.

Experiments with animals have shown that addiction to drugs such as morphine, and subsequent withdrawal symptoms, may also be conditioned. Rats who have been administered increasing doses of morphine which are always signalled by distinctive environmental cues come to tolerate doses that would previously have been lethal. The same animals will die, however, if given an identical dose in the presence of quite different environmental cues. It appears that the usual cues become a CS for conditioned homeostatic reactions which oppose the drug effects, and it is these compensatory CRs which constitute tolerance. In the absence of the CS signalling drug onset, a compensatory CR does not occur, and the animal reacts as if receiving morphine for the first time. The same phenomenon can explain why human addicts experience most craving and withdrawal effects in the presence of stimuli that typically precede drug use.

Experimental neuroses

If animals are fed following one signal (CS+) but not after another similar signal (CS−), conditioning of salivation will occur only to the first. If CS+ and CS− are then made progressively more similar, so that the animals have difficulty in discriminating between them, the conditioned reactions may be suddenly lost even if the original CS+ is again presented. Some animals treated in this way show signs of emotional distress or exhibit stereotyped and apparently meaningless behaviours. Similar phenomena have also been described when a behaviour has been both rewarded and punished in the past, resulting in a so-called *approach-avoidance conflict*. Although labelled '*experimental neuroses*' it is not certain that these behaviours arise in the same way as do human neuroses (see Chapter 9).

It is clear, however, that conditioning can result in extremely persistent anxiety or fear reactions. If a signal is paired with unpleasant stimuli such as severe electric shocks then under some circumstances the conditioned fear reaction to the CS alone can be very difficult to extinguish (see avoidance learning below).

Operant conditioning

Operant conditioning was originally studied in animals by B.F.

Skinner, and his name is still associated with this learning paradigm. His studies showed that the probability of performing a simple response is systematically related to the proportion of occasions on which that response has previously been rewarded. For example, a rat will learn to press a lever which delivers a single food pellet on every press and will continue to operate the lever at a steady rate as long as the animal remains hungry.

A behaviour (such as pressing the bar) is described as an operant response whenever the probability of that behaviour occurring again depends on its consequences (in this case the delivery of food). The consequences of a behaviour are said to be *reinforcing* if the probability of that response occurring again increases, or *punishing* if the probability of the response decreases. Reinforcement is not quite the same as reward, since the probability of the rat pressing the lever will also be increased if this has the effect of turning off an unpleasant stimulus such as an electric shock (negative reinforcement). The fact that removal of shock increases the response probability means that it is defined as reinforcing rather than punishing.

Particular *schedules of reinforcement* or punishment have sometimes been found to lead to unexpected results. If animals are initially reinforced for every response, then every other response, then every third and so on, the rate of responding accelerates rather than remaining steady or slowing down. Furthermore, although the complete removal of reinforcement leads to eventual extinction of an operant response, the intermittent schedule described above markedly delays this extinction process.

Operant learning in humans can be illustrated by the behaviour of children who are ignored by their mother except when misbehaving. Since attention from the mother normally reinforces the behaviour which it follows, such children may begin to misbehave more frequently. Inadvertent operant learning of this kind is thought to underlie some forms of behaviour disorders.

Shaping operant behaviour

Very complex responses can be gradually built up by the process known as *shaping*, in which successive approximations to a new behaviour are reinforced. In the example above, if the mother becomes exasperated and pays less attention to the child, then a more extreme example of misbehaviour may be necessary before it is again reinforced by her attention. The end result of this process may be that the mother inadvertently shapes the child towards more serious forms of misbehaviour such as temper tantrums or destructiveness. More usually shaping produces desirable and socially adaptive behaviours, as when parents selectively reinforce early attempts at language or toileting with attention or praise.

Teaching self-help skills to the handicapped

Shaping is used systematically with mentally handicapped children who have failed to acquire normal self-care behaviours. Each behaviour (e.g. dressing oneself) is broken down into simple steps that can be reinforced and then combined into the complete behaviour that is desired. When inadvertent shaping has resulted in undesirable behaviour (e.g. repeated self-injury in mentally handicapped individuals) it may be necessary to use extinction methods — systematically removing attention whenever the undesirable behaviour occurs. Alternatively, it may be useful to reinforce behaviour that is incompatible with the undesired habit, with punishment used only as the last resort.

Avoidance learning

A child attacked by a dog at an early age may not only come to fear all dogs (generalisation of conditioned fear) but also seek to avoid them in the future. Because avoidance of a conditioned stimulus for fear is reinforcing in itself, any avoidance behaviour may become stronger over time rather than weaker.

Such avoidance will effectively minimise the amount of contact with the CS (e.g. sight of dogs). However, without exposure to the CS extinction of a conditioned response is extremely slow, so that the fear will tend to persist. Experiments with animals have shown that conditioned fear reactions of this sort can be successfully extinguished by systematic exposure to the feared CS while avoidance is prevented, and that this process is accelerated by the simultaneous presentation of reinforcement for approach behaviour. Such experiments have led to the development of related methods for treating human phobias, which will be discussed later (see Chapter 9).

MODELLING

Modelling is the term given to learning that consists of the imitation

of behaviour observed in others. For example, experiments have shown that children are more likely to behave aggressively after they have observed another acting in an aggressive fashion, particularly if that behaviour was successful (i.e. was reinforced). Summarising the results of many such studies, behaviour is more likely to be imitated if the models involved are:
(a) perceived as similar to the observer, and
(b) liked or admired by the observer.

Children are thought to be particularly likely to model themselves on the same-sex parent. Beliefs and attitudes may be adopted in this way as well as behaviours. For example, girls are more likely to model themselves on their mothers, and are more likely than boys to be rewarded for female *sex role behaviours* (behaviours more typical of women than of men).

Modelling and illness

Complaint of abdominal pain in children is a common paediatric problem, although organic disease is found in only a minority of cases. Parents of children who commonly complain of such pains tend themselves to be preoccupied with illness, and consequently attend closely to their children's symptoms. 'Illness behaviour' can thus be learned in two ways: (1) parents may provide a model of illness concern that is adopted by the child, and (2) the child's verbal complaints may then be reinforced by attention. Similarly, dental fear in childhood is related not only to painful experiences at the dentist, but also to the presence of fearful attitudes in parents.

Modelling as treatment

Modelling can also be used to reverse some adverse effects of early learning. For example, a fear of hospitals in children can be reduced by viewing a film in which other children are shown overcoming their fear while undergoing a range of medical procedures (see the section in Chapter 6 on preparation for surgery). A number of studies have shown that the procedure known as *participant modelling* is particularly effective in overcoming specific phobias. Phobic clients first observe others gradually entering the feared situation and learning to cope with it, and then imitate the same behaviour themselves (see Fig. 3.5 and Chapter 8).

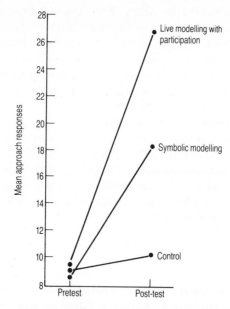

Fig. 3.5 Treatment of snake phobia: mean score on a behavioural test before and after different treatments (maximum score — 28 — would mean picking up and handling a harmless snake) (from Bandura et al 1969).

FURTHER READING

Baddeley A 1982 Your memory: a users guide. Penguin, Harmondsworth
Broadbent D, Weiskrantz L 1982 The neuropsychology of cognitive function. The Royal Society, London
Davey G 1981 Applications of conditioning theory. Psychology in progress. Methuen, London

STUDY QUESTIONS

1. Define: conditioned stimulus and response, extinction, generalisation, reinforcement, punishment, shaping, modelling, memory span, primacy effect, anterograde amnesia.
2. Is the 'bell and pad' treatment of enuresis an example of classical conditioning or operant learning?
3. What operant-learning principles are used in the management of the mentally handicapped?
4. What learning methods have been used to reduce fear?
5. What reasons are there to believe that there are several processes involved in memory?
6. What factors increase or decrease the probability that patients will remember medical advice?

4

Psychology and the lifespan

CHILD DEVELOPMENT

The study of development in infants and children is an important aspect of psychology, and also has numerous implications for clinical care. In the present day, over 20% of the population of England and Wales are aged less than 15, and many of the problems in children brought to medical attention concern behaviour or the development of abilities. Despite large variations between individuals, development tends to follow an orderly sequence. The *developmental trajectory* in the case of short term memory is illustrated in Figure 4.1, where the progressive enlargement of digit span with increasing age is shown. The relatively fixed sequence makes it possible to use standardised tests when assessing whether an individual child is proceeding satisfactorily. Performance on particular functions (motor, language, etc.) can be checked against age-related norms to calculate the child's position in relation to its peers.

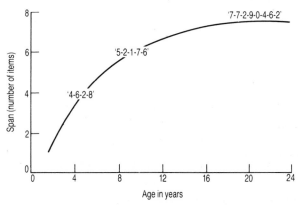

Fig. 4.1 Changes in digit span with age. The number of items a child is able to repeat accurately develops with age to a maximum of seven or eight items (from Fischer & Lazerson 1984).

Genetic factors

The role played by genetic factors in determining behaviour and ability has been debated hotly for many decades, particularly in respect of intelligence and personality (see Chapter 5). There are hereditary conditions such as Huntington's chorea in which a direct effect of genetic endowment on mental deterioration in adulthood can be seen. However, in most cases genetic and environmental factors collaborate in development. Even a genetic defect such as phenylketonuria (PKU), which leads to mental retardation, is only expressed within a certain nutritional environment, and can be reversed with a diet low in phenylalanine. The rate of sensorimotor development is also determined by an interaction of environment and heredity, since the acquisition of co-ordinated body movements such as walking can be brought forward with appropriate training.

Prenatal influences on development

There is growing evidence that maternal behaviour and experience affect development. Malnutrition during pregnancy may lead to premature birth and low birth weight, while adverse effects on neuronal development of the fetal brain have been observed in animals. Cigarette smoking during pregnancy has been associated with low birth weight, which in turn may put the infant at a disadvantage developmentally. Heavy alcohol consumption may lead to *fetal alcohol syndrome* in which retarded growth and facial abnormalities are present, together with disturbances of central nervous system function.

Stress in pregnancy

High levels of maternal anxiety or psychosocial stress may be associated with complications of pregnancy and delivery. One study found a higher incidence of major life events, particularly in the third trimester, among mothers giving birth prematurely or to low birth weight infants. Nuckolls and co-workers showed that the effects of life stress on pregnancy complications were buffered by the presence of social supports. The results in Figure 4.2 indicate that high levels of life stress were associated with complications, but only when social supports were poor. The mechanism underlying this pattern is not clear, but may relate to the release of stress hormones, and also to increased rates of smoking or poor nutrition among those experiencing life events (see Chapters 6 and 7).

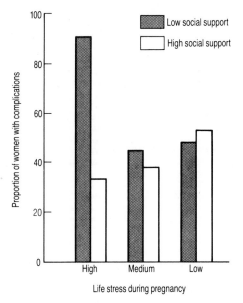

Fig. 4.2 Complications of pregnancy in women with high life-change scores before pregnancy who then experience high, medium or low stress during pregnancy (from Nuckolls et al 1972).

Early motor development

New-born infants show a number of reflex behaviours (fixed patterns elicited by specific stimuli) such as the sucking, grasping and rooting reflexes, which form the basis for later action patterns. Other reflexes such as crying and smiling may serve to stimulate adults into caring for the infant. Within a few hours, learned responses such as head turning or sucking at different rates can be acquired through operant conditioning. Objects can soon be located through the senses of sight and hearing, and within the first weeks the baby can imitate an adult by sticking out its tongue. The sequence of development is orderly, although the age at which behaviours are acquired varies greatly. This is illustrated in Figure 4.3.

Perceptual development

Patterned visual stimulation is essential for the development of visually guided behaviour (see Chapter 1). Experiments by Hein & Held indicate that active use of visual experience is also

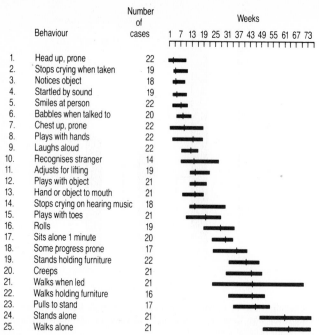

	Behaviour	Number of cases
1.	Head up, prone	22
2.	Stops crying when taken	19
3.	Notices object	18
4.	Startled by sound	19
5.	Smiles at person	22
6.	Babbles when talked to	20
7.	Chest up, prone	22
8.	Plays with hands	22
9.	Laughs aloud	22
10.	Recognises stranger	14
11.	Adjusts for lifting	19
12.	Plays with object	21
13.	Hand or object to mouth	21
14.	Stops crying on hearing music	18
15.	Plays with toes	21
16.	Rolls	19
17.	Sits alone 1 minute	20
18.	Some progress prone	17
19.	Stands holding furniture	22
20.	Creeps	21
21.	Walks when led	21
22.	Walks holding furniture	16
23.	Pulls to stand	17
24.	Stands alone	21
25.	Walks alone	21

Fig. 4.3 Sequence of motor development (From *Development in Infancy* 2/E by T. G. R. Bower. Copyright © 1974, 1982 W. H. Freeman and Company. Reprinted with permission.)

necessary. Kittens were placed in tandem in a carousel apparatus so that while one member of the pair moved actively, the other was carried about passively. Although both received the same perceptual experience, active animals showed superior perception of space and depth.

Infants prefer looking at patterns rather than blank fields after a few weeks, and by about 3 months prefer to look at faces rather than jumbled patterns. At this age, however, they always cannot recognise specific faces. Such recognition usually occurs between 6 and 9 months, when a fear of strangers also develops. Depth perception is present at 2 to 3 months, but is not completely integrated with behaviour until some time later.

Environmental 'enrichment'

The effects of levels of stimulation in early life on later abilities and brain function have been studied in rats. Following weaning, rats were either placed in single cages (impoverished environment) or

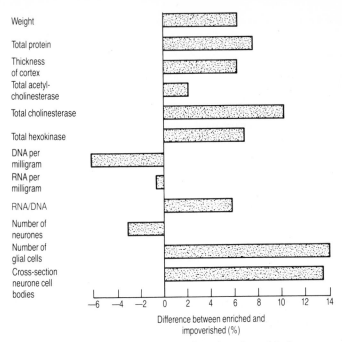

Fig. 4.4 Differences in the occipital cortex of rats kept in enriched or impoverished environments from 25–105 days (From Rosenzweig et al 1972. Reproduced with permission from Scientific American.)

else were raised in large cages with other rats, numerous toys and interesting objects. Rats reared in the enriched environment later showed superior performance on behavioural tasks. The experience also had an influence on brain anatomy. This is shown in Figure 4.4. On average, rats reared in enriched environments had heavier, thicker occipital cortex, and the neurone cell bodies were larger.

The effects of enriched environments on human development have also been studied, by comparing infants given toys in their cots, patterned sheets and opportunities to look around the room with those raised in dull institutional cots. Although this treatment promotes visually directed behaviour, development cannot be accelerated beyond maturational level. Very high levels of stimulation may even have deleterious effects on development.

SOCIAL AND PERSONAL DEVELOPMENT

There are wide variations in the behaviour of neonates. Some show regular patterns of eating and sleeping and adapt positively to

Table 4.1 Temperamental qualities in infancy

Activity level	— tendency to be in physical motion
Rhythmicity	— regularity of biological functions
Approach or withdrawal	— initial reaction to any new stimulation
Adaptability	— flexibility of behaviour following initial reaction
Intensity of reaction	— energy level of responses
Threshold of responsiveness	— intensity of stimulus required to produce reaction
Quality of mood	— proportion of happy, friendly to unhappy, unfriendly behaviour
Distractability	— degree to which extraneous stimulation disrupts ongoing behaviour
Attention span and persistence	— length of time activities are maintained and tolerance of difficulty

From Thomas et al (1970).

changes in the environment, while others are irregular, withdraw from new objects and are often irritable. A study by Thomas et al (1970) indicated that some differences in infant *temperament* persisted even when the children were at school. The nine temperamental qualities listed in Table 4.1 continued to be detectable in the behaviour of 10-year-olds. These variations may be related to personality differences in adult life (see Chapter 5).

Social attachments become more specific over the first few months of life, so that in the second 6 months the infant develops fear of strangers and distress at separation from care takers. The infant is said to use the parent as a 'secure base' from which to explore the world, making short expeditions to examine new objects but returning frequently for comfort. Later, children learn to separate themselves mentally from parents in the process of *individuation*, transferring some of their social needs to their peers. Difficulties in making this transition may result in problems such as separation anxiety, in which children remain fearful of leaving their mothers.

Mother–infant separation

The notion that separation from the mother early in life (maternal deprivation) has profound effects on later development was propagated by the psychoanalyst John Bowlby. He argued that adequate mothering involved a warm unbroken attachment to one person within the child's own family. In the absence of such a background the child would fail to develop bonds in later life and would also be vulnerable to psychiatric disorders. This view was supported in the 1950s and 1960s by studies of language retardation in children raised in institutions, and the high incidence of delinquency in children from 'broken homes'.

More recent work indicates that this view is incorrect. Children are capable of forming a number of different attachments, and the psychological effects of institutional rearing are not negative if alternative relationships are allowed to develop. The retarded development of children raised in poor institutions results in part from the lack of stimulation and attention to individual needs. Improvements in institutional care have been shown to promote intellectual and language development.

There is also considerable evidence that the children of working women are not at increased risk for delinquency or psychiatric disorder. The association between broken homes and later disturbance depends on the long term level of discord in the household prior to separation, rather than the separation itself. Death of a parent does not in itself lead to raised risk of adolescent disturbance, even though in this case separation is permanent. It may, however, increase the likelihood of depression in adult life (see Chapter 9).

Hospitalisation of children

Hospitalisation is one of the most common causes of separation from parents. No ill effects are seen in children younger than about 6 months, but from this age until about 4 years the child may experience considerable distress. Three phases are seen: protest, withdrawal, then emotional detachment. A study in British hospitals by Douglas (1975) showed that children in this age band who were separated for more than 2 weeks were at increased risk for behavioural and educational disturbances later on in school.

However, this pattern is influenced by many factors, notably the temperament of the child and the quality of the previous mother–infant relationship. Less distress is found in children who have a good relationship with their parents. Separation distress can also be reduced by substitute maternal care, while extra stimulation may be needed to replace the level provided at home. Distress due to separation is often accompanied by worry about medical or surgical procedures, and discomfort resulting from the child's medical condition. Methods of preparing children psychologically for medical procedures are described in Chapter 6. In some modern hospitals, parents are able to move in with the child so as to avoid the distress of separation.

Child abuse

It is estimated that two children a week die of injuries inflicted by their parents in England and Wales, and many more suffer to a lesser, while still severe, extent as a result of physical or emotional abuse. Precise estimates of the prevalence of child abuse are difficult to obtain, since many minor cases never come to the attention of medical or legal professionals, and other cases are passed off by parents as accidental. In those cases which do come to light, either because parents seek help or because the abuse is difficult to conceal, surveys have suggested that certain features may be characteristic.

Most physical abuse is of young children (below the age of 5 years) and is usually carried out by mothers, probably because they have much more time in contact with the child, although fathers may be involved in more serious cases. Abusing parents are typically young, ill prepared for parenthood, and were more likely to have been abused themselves as children. Children at risk tend to be difficult to cope with, and may have been premature or unhealthy, which can prevent a close bond forming between mother and child. Most abuse occurs during times of emotional distress for the parents, and is often triggered by some disliked behaviour in the child such as persistent crying. If detected early, further child abuse problems can be prevented by helping parents to cope with emotional stress in other ways, and teaching them better methods of child management.

Sex roles

The development of sex roles is an example of *socialisation*, where the behaviour patterns and values of adults are acquired by children. Behaviours typical of each sex tend to be learned in the preschool years, with sex-appropriate toys and play activities. Girls may be encouraged to inhibit aggression and to be passive while boistrous behaviour is tolerated in boys. Boys are discouraged from playing with dolls and domestic toys, and future expectations are instilled in role-playing games (e.g. doctor-and-nurse). The influence of early socialisation makes it difficult to determine the extent to which later differences in attitudes and behaviour have a genetic basis. However, because some differences appear in almost every culture they are quite likely to have a partly genetic basis. These are: greater aggression in males and more nurturance in females, better verbal ability in girls, better spatial and number ability in adult men.

COGNITIVE AND SPEECH DEVELOPMENT

The Swiss scientist Jean Piaget argued that children passed through four periods of cognitive development characterised by different forms of thought and knowledge: the sensorimotor phase (0–2 years), the pre-operational phase (ages 2–7), the concrete-operational phase (ages 7–11) and finally the adult logical-formal operational phase. These periods were said to be qualitatively distinct, with abrupt rather than gradual transitions between them.

An example of a cognitive pattern that changes during development is the child's ability to take someone else's perspective or point of view. Piaget argued that until the later stages of the pre-operational phase, children are *egocentric*, and cannot perceive that another person's experience of the world is different from their own. This has been tested with a three-dimensional model of a mountain range, in which a doll is placed in different locations. The child is permitted to look round the model, and is then asked what the doll would see from its position. Children of 5 or 6 years are unable to 'see' the model from the doll's point of view, but instead select their own perspective. However this ability changes abruptly as the child grows older. Other examples are the conservation of objects and volume, and at later stages the ability to think logically without contradictions.

Piaget's theories were derived largely from observation of his own children, and more recent studies indicate that the typical pattern is more complex. Piaget may have overestimated the limitations of thinking and problem solving said to exist at different ages, for later experiments show that many of these effects depend on the precise environmental context in which they are tested. For example, 4-year-old children can share another person's perspective if they are tested in different ways. The theory that thought progresses towards an adult ideal of coherent logic is not consistent with evidence concerning problem-solving errors in adults (see Chapter 10). Alternative views suggest that development is more continuous, that different modes of thought may exist simultaneously and that advances in particular types of cognitive ability will occur with appropriate training or the acquisition of specific skills.

Acquisition of language

The dictionary definition of an infant is 'one who cannot speak', and language acquisition is a crucial developmental process. Children do imitate adult speech and are often reinforced for their utterances, but systematic observation shows that this cannot completely account for language acquisition. Although the timing of speech production is variable, most children pass through the same sequence, and this is illustrated in Figure 4.5. Such findings suggest that the human brain is to some extent preprogrammed to acquire speech at certain stages of development. Language acquisition is an interactive process, and parents aid learning by such things as repetition (and correction) of the child's utterances, emphasis on key words in a particular situation, and expansion of short phrases into the complete adult form. However, children also learn *grammatical rules* that they have not been explicitly taught. For example they learn that plurals are made by adding 's' and the

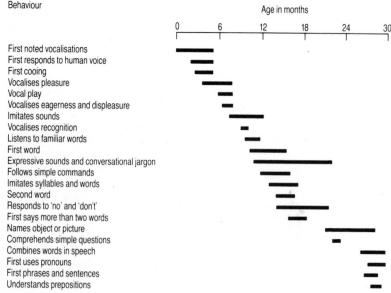

Fig. 4.5 Sequence of language development (Reprinted with permission, from *Development and Growth and Ageing*, Carter (1980), published by Croom Helm.)

past is indicated by adding 'ed', as indicated by errors such as 'sheeps' and 'finded', which they could not have copied.

There may be a critical *sensitive period* for the learning of language, lasting until the age of 8–10 years. Following this period language acquisition may be impaired, as in the rare cases of children raised in isolation or found living wild who are subsequently taught some speech. The sensitive period may coincide with the development of lateralisation of function in the two cerebral hemispheres, and is also consistent with the effects of brain damage at different ages (see Chapter 1).

Childhood autism

Autism is a very rare and puzzling disorder (affecting less than one in a thousand) which may develop in apparently normal infants some time before the age of 3 years. Its most characteristic feature is a severe communication difficulty, in which children avoid eye contact or other forms of social exchange, and fail to develop normal speech. Many simply imitate what is said to them without any sign of understanding (*echolalia*), although other abilities may be less affected, and a few autistic children develop unusually good numerical, musical or artistic skills. Common behavioural problems include the frequent repetition of apparently meaningless actions, and displays of intense distress if they are interrupted or familiar surroundings are disturbed.

Those who eventually develop a simple but useful level of speech (approximately half of all cases) may be able to live independent lives, while the remainder usually remain under institutional care. Special educational programmes are used to help normalise their speech and behaviour, based partly on operant learning and modelling techniques. Although the cause of autism remains unknown, the pattern of symptoms suggests failure in some aspect of brain function subserving language development.

BEHAVIOURAL PROBLEMS OF CHILDHOOD

Apart from the very rare psychotic conditions of childhood, the common problems of development can be conveniently divided into mental handicap (Chapter 5), developmental delays of a more specific kind, and other emotional or behavioural disturbances. In a recent survey of 700 3-year-olds in a London suburb, approximately 7% were found to have moderate or severe behavioural problems — 9% of boys and 5% of girls. Here is a description of a fairly severe problem from this survey (Richman et al 1982).

Peter is reported to be very wild, and totally out of control, having a tantrum whenever he is frustrated. He torments his 9-month-old brother so that he cannot be left with him. He has a poor appetite, is faddy, and takes a long time to settle at night. He worries that his mother might die, and is also frightened of 'monsters' and of noises at night. He frequently shouts and screams, and the neighbours and other children will not have anything to do with him.

Particularly high rates of behavioural problems were found in deprived and disharmonious families with many children, living in high density areas such as tower blocks of flats. Later follow-up when the children were 8 years old revealed that those who had shown marked problems at 3 years continued to be disturbed in later childhood.

Statistical analysis of symptom patterns in such older children shows clearly that there are two underlying clusters of symptoms: emotional disturbance (e.g. excessive fearfulness and lack of confidence), and conduct disorder (e.g. restlessness, temper tantrums, etc.). This suggests that the symptoms may reflect more fundamental dimensions of personality such as emotionality and introversion–extraversion (see Chapter 5). In the sample of children discussed above there were rather more conduct problems than other emotional disturbances, but this was entirely accounted for by the larger proportion of boys displaying antisocial conduct. Later on in life, women have a higher frequency of emotional or neurotic disorders, while delinquent behaviour remains predominantly a male problem.

Management of behaviour problems

Conduct and neurotic types of problem require different treatment approaches. In some ways, excessive fearfulness in children resembles adult phobic and anxiety states, and may respond to the same approach. School phobias, for example, in which children are afraid to leave home and go to school, can best be treated by gradual and reassuring exposure to the various aspects of school that elicit fear and avoidance. School phobia is sometimes accompanied by anxiety about being away from mother or home (separation anxiety), so that family involvement in the treatment programmes is often helpful.

School phobia is to be distinguished from truancy, which does not arise from fear, but is associated with other rebellious and antisocial behaviour. Such conduct problems are more difficult to treat, but some success has been achieved by helping parents to set firm guidelines for acceptable behaviour, and the consistent use of social approval for adherence to these limits, while using extinction methods (such as 'time out') for infractions. Parents of aggressive boys have been found to use physical punishment methods more often than other families, and also tend to model or indirectly reinforce aggressive acts either by showing approval for them or by giving way to demands. The treatment of conduct disorder thus also involves changing the behaviour and child management methods of parents.

Developmental delay and learning disabilities

Many childhood problems arise from delays or deficits in specific developmental functions, such as control of elimination or the acquisition of language skills. The timing of bladder and bowel control is very variable, so that about 40% of children are dry at night by the age of 2 years, and almost 90% by the age of 5. Persistence of enuresis beyond this age is usually considered a problem, and can be treated with the bell and pad alarm method (see Chapter 3). Encopresis (involuntary defaecation during the day) is much less common, with an incidence of 1–2% at the age of 8 years. Treatment for this more embarrassing problem is usually via positive retraining methods, using encouragement and social reward for normal toileting behaviour.

Developmental dyslexia

One of the best-studied learning disabilities is that of developmental dyslexia: a specific difficulty in learning to read and write. The condition varies in form from simple educational and motivational failure to a relatively clear neurological problem. Figure 4.6 shows a 9-year-old dyslexic child's copy of a cube and a bicycle, and reveals an obvious perceptual–motor defect.

More commonly, dyslexia is associated with mirror reversals, so that the letters 'b' and 'd' are confused, as might be the words 'was' and 'saw'. More dyslexic than normal children are left handed, and may show other signs of incomplete brain lateralisation, suggesting that the language function of the dominant hemisphere is less well established in dyslexia (see Chapter 1).

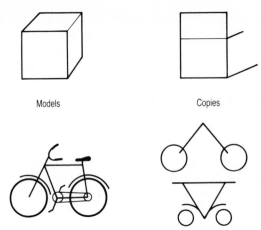

Models   Copies

Fig. 4.6 Attempts by a dyslexic 9-year-old to reproduce drawings of a cube and a bicycle (From *Human Development* by Kurt W. Fischer and Arlyne Lazerson. Copyright © 1984. Reprinted with the permission of W. H. Freeman and Company.)

PSYCHOLOGICAL EFFECTS OF AGEING

As we grow older, characteristic changes occur in cognitive, emotional and social functions. The elderly are typically more cautious and introverted, while also becoming increasingly susceptible to emotional disorders. Because old people are often reticent about their problems, and such difficulties are seen by others as inevitable, treatable conditions are often ignored. Changes in social role associated with retirement and with the departure of younger family members lead to changes in lifestyle which may remove major sources of satisfaction and reduce feelings of self-worth. Life events such as physical disease, handicap or bereavement increase the likelihood of depressive disorders, and the risk of suicide. Even in the absence of major life events, all elderly people must cope with deficits such as a deteriorating memory, reduced sensory acuity and loss of physical strength. For these reasons, while old age can be a time of fulfilment, this tends to be so only in those who adapt well to life change and who have maintained leisure-time interests and hobbies.

Cognitive changes in the elderly

Peak performance on intellectual tasks actually occurs relatively early in life, particularly for abilities that require mental speed or the acquisition of new material. Tests of reasoning or psychomotor speed show a peak at around 30 years, followed by a slow decline which accelerates after the age of 60, although verbal abilities may continue to rise through middle age and then decline slowly or not at all (see Figure 5.2). Similarly, ageing is accompanied by a steady loss of efficiency in the recall of newly learned material, which starts in early adulthood. However, it is important to realise that the ability to acquire new information remains good when learning is carried out under optimal conditions, for example if the rate of presentation is slow, and the new information is associated with older material already in memory. As was indicated in Chapter 3, memory loss does not always mean that information is not encoded, but often results from a failure of retrieval. By increasing the number of associations between old and new information, or by providing reminders to aid the retrieval process, the ability of old people to remember can be much improved.

Recall of medical advice

Memory for medical advice is a special problem with elderly patients, since they may be receiving treatment for several conditions, but are also more easily confused. For this reason, presentation of medical advice to elderly patients in simple categorised form (see Chapter 3) is obviously particularly important. However, one of the most common memory failures in elderly people is that of forgetting whether they have or have not already performed a familiar act, such as taking a pill (or telling their family an often-repeated story!). To overcome this problem, a tear-off calendar may be used which indicates when the last pill was taken or when the next is due. This simple method has been shown to reduce the usual high rate of potentially dangerous medical errors in the elderly to a relatively low and safe level.

Diseases of old age

More than 25% of people admitted to hospital are over 60 years of age, and this proportion is steadily growing as the proportion of elderly people in the general population continues to increase.

Approximately 10% of all those over 65 years shown signs of organic brain disease (or dementia) which cannot be reversed by physical treatment. For these reasons, it is inevitable that medical practice in the future will become increasingly concerned with the elderly patient.

Within hospitals or other institutions, elderly patients are often subjected to what amounts to sensory deprivation, since there is little to occupy them intellectually or socially. As a result, surveys of long stay wards have shown that most patients become progressively less and less active. Provision of even very simple occupational therapy materials is sufficient to increase activity and social engagement. There are good reasons to believe that such procedures may maintain physical as well as psychological health. In one experiment with residents of an old people's home, half were randomly given responsibility for activities, timetables and so on, while the other half had all such decisions made for them by the staff. On later follow-up it was found that a significantly higher proportion of residents who had decisions made for them had died.

Dementia and Alzheimer's disease

The physical changes which occur in ageing are well known, and include loss of skin elasticity, muscular atrophy and deterioration in flexibility of limbs. There are also changes in the structure of the brain, with progressive loss of neurones, reduced cerebral blood flow and oxygen consumption. Alzheimer's disease is the best-established dementing process, and is associated with accelerated intellectual deterioration, together with specific neuronal changes such as the development of neurofibrillary tangles in the brain.

In the absence of any physical treatment capable of reversing this degenerative process, good psychological management and support are extremely important in slowing deterioration and preserving the quality of life. Much of the characteristic confusion and disorientation of the Alzheimer's patient appears to result from an exaggerated form of the memory deficit which occurs in normal ageing. Specific methods used to ameliorate the effects of this deficit include reality orientation, in which patients are provided with constant written reminders of where they are, what time it is and what they should be doing. This method has been shown to be effective in reducing behavioural signs of confusion and disorientation, but long term benefits depend on a continuing programme of support.

FURTHER READING

Fischer K W, Lazerson A 1984 Human development. W H Freeman, Oxford
Whitehead A 1984 Psychological intervention in dementia. In: Kay D, Burrows

G (eds) Handbook of studies on psychiatry and old age. Elsevier Science, Amsterdam.
Yule W 1985 Childhood disorders. In: Bradley B P, Thompson C (eds) Psychological applications in psychiatry. Wiley, Chichester

STUDY QUESTIONS

1. Describe the main types of psychological disorder seen in children.
2. What cognitive changes take place after the age of 60 years, and what can be done to reduce their impact?
3. What are the consequences of social and emotional deprivation in childhood for later development?
4. How does an understanding of normal child development assist in the management of developmental disorders?
5. Is temperament in infancy relevant to later behaviour?
6. What factors are thought to influence the cognitive development of children?

5

Individual differences in ability and behaviour

It is obvious that people vary greatly in their abilities, and in the ways they feel or behave. We usually refer to these variations as differences in intelligence or personality. However, although our language is full of words used to describe individual differences, this does not prove that such characteristics actually exit — they may after all only reflect our own prejudice or ignorance about human behaviour. For example, a doctor having difficulty in understanding why a patient resists taking medication might simply label that individual as 'uncooperative', although the patient's behaviour may in fact arise from a misunderstanding or a view of disease that is different from the doctor's. Such intuitive judgements of personality tend to be dominated by first impressions, which then persist and colour later judgements. These impressions are often based on non-verbal cues (e.g. eye contact, posture, facial expression and so on) that may have little real relationship to the personality judgements that we arrive at.

Reliability and validity of personality measures

In order to place the study of individual differences on to a scientific footing, we need first to define objectively the personality variations that are thought to exist. Secondly, it is necessary to develop a reliable method of measuring any particular characteristic along a dimension or scale.

Reliability in this context refers to a statistic providing an indication of how closely two or more assessments of the same personality characteristic are in agreement. If reliability is low, and two separate administrations of the same test give different results, then the test is not likely to be of much use in measuring personality. The measure of agreement most commonly used is the *correlation coefficient*. This is a statistic that varies from 1.0, indicating perfect agreement, through 0.0, indicating no agreement or disagreement, to −1.0, indicating complete disagreement. A good test should have a reliability of 0.8 or more.

One possible reason for reliability being low is that the test is too subjective, and testers cannot agree on the outcome. Methods such as the Rorschach (ink-blot) test that involve reactions to ambiguous pictures tend to suffer from this problem. Another possible reason for low reliability is that people are genuinely inconsistent in their behaviour from situation to situation. Such inconsistency is probably rather greater than is commonly assumed, but personality tests are none the less expected to measure whatever behavioural consistencies do exist.

A *personality trait* (or specific characteristic that varies from person to person) is thus defined as a distinguishable and relatively enduring way in which one individual consistently differs from another. Since tests of personality traits (e.g. extraversion) often take the form of questionnaires in which people describe their own behaviour, it is also important that such tests really do measure the relevant behaviour.

Validity is the name given to the extent to which tests truly measure what they purport to measure. Intelligence tests, for example, should be able to predict (at least partly) how well a child will do at school, or whether an adult can succeed in an intellectually demanding job. In contrast to established objective tests, casual impressions about people can often be quite invalid. For example, patients judged by doctors as being unlikely to follow medical advice turn out to be just as likely to comply as others are (see Chapter 11).

INTELLIGENCE

Early in this century, the French Government asked a psychologist (Alfred Binet) to devise a way of predicting which children were too slow to profit from normal schooling. His solution, first published in 1905, gave rise to what we now call intelligence (or IQ) tests. A large number of questions and problems were collected in order to assess mental abilities such as verbal comprehension, memory and perceptual speed (see Table 5.1 for example items). Based on the idea that abilities steadily increase with age, Binet selected and ordered the items by difficulty, that is, according to the first age at which children could perform them successfully. A 5-year-old child who could just succeed with all the items passed by the average 6-year-old (for example) could thus be said to have

Table 5.1 Sample IQ items

1. Height is to width as tall is to: short, large, broad, small.
2. Which shape could fit over the first one if turned round without leaving the paper:
3. What number comes next in the series: 1, 3, 7, 15, 31, . . .

a *mental age* of 6. In later versions, the intelligent quotient (IQ) was developed, as defined in the following equation:

$$IQ = \frac{\text{mental age}}{\text{chronological age}} \times 100$$

The above method of calculating IQ is no longer used, since defining higher intelligence as being ahead for one's age is not always satisfactory. Development does not always progress smoothly, and the formula breaks down completely in the case of adults. Instead, IQ is now calculated using the distribution of scores on a full range of mental tasks across a large sample of people in each specific age group. The mean of all scores in each age group is set at 100, and the standard deviation is set at 15 (see Fig. 5.1). An individual's score is then expressed in terms of its position in the distribution for other individuals of the same age. This has the advantage that any IQ score can be easily converted into the percentage of the population of that age who score above or below that point. For example, about 95% of the population obtain IQ scores between 70 (two standard deviations below the mean) and 130 (two standard deviations above the mean) across all ages. It is important to remember that an IQ value is meaningless

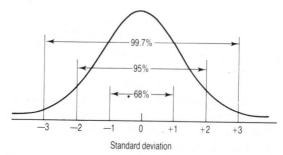

Fig. 5.1 The normal curve showing divisions by standard deviation (SD). The area under the curve indicates the population frequency of any score, or range of scores. For example, IQ range 85–115 covers one SD above and below the mean, and includes 68% of the population.

unless the standard deviation is known so that this conversion into population percentiles can be performed.

Mental handicap

Intelligence tests are commonly used to assess the degree of mental handicap, to help with educational decisions in children or management problems with handicapped adults. Children with IQ scores of 75 or below are normally thought to need special educational help, and those with IQs below 50 will probably need more general institutional care (see Table 5.2).

Table 5.2 Implications of ability levels in mental handicap

IQ	% of pop.	Probable ability as adult
50–70	1.6	Equivalent to 8–12-year-old: with help may be able to support themselves in the community.
30–50	0.3	Equivalent to 4–7-year-old: dependent on institutional support. May speak reasonably but read little or not at all.
30 or less	0.1	Equivalent to 4-year-old or less: totally dependent on institution. Limited as no self-care and speech.

At higher IQ levels (50–75) specific organic pathology is rare, and abilities depend more on interaction between genetic endowment and social environment (discussed later). At lower levels (below 50) the probability of specific pathological conditions becomes greater. In a study of mentally handicapped patients with IQ less than 50, 21% were found to be suffering from a genetically determined disorder (of whom 16% were Down's syndrome), 4% had hydrocephalus, 24% had suffered damage from external causes, and 51% could not be classified.

Poor social environment can in extreme cases produce a picture of severe mental handicap, but fortunately this is usually reversible. For example, a pair of twins were rescued from conditions of semi-isolation, cruelty and malnutrition at the age of 7 years. They were abnormally fearful, had little speech, and measured IQ levels were in the 40s. Some years later, after adoption and with special social and educational help, their IQ had risen to the mid 90s and they were able to manage in normal schools despite being rather backward scholastically.

Genetic and environmental influences on ability

The above account clearly illustrates the adverse effects of environmental deprivation, although such severe cases are fortunately rare. More generally, it seems that there are genetic limits on intellectual level, but that the full development and expression of this ability are also determined by rearing in favourable or unfavourable environments.

Although heredity and environment cannot be considered separately, under normal conditions about three-quarters of the variation in IQ is thought to be attributable to differences in genetic endowment. This estimate is based on data on twins, which show that the similarity of IQ scores depends more on closeness of genetic relationship than on specific home environment. The IQ scores of identical twins reared together tend to be closer (correlation of about 0.9) than those of similar twins reared apart (about 0.7). Although this small difference does show the effect of environment, all these correlations are far higher than those for unrelated children who are reared together (about 0.2).

Needless to say, the amount of variation attributable to environmental influences can be greater than this in the case of disadvantaged ethnic or socially deprived groups. Another problem arises from the fact that IQ tests were designed for those brought up and educated in our own culture; they may be quite inappropriate for other cultural groups.

The development of intelligence

Most mental abilities increase rapidly up to the age of about 16 years, and then remain approximately stable before declining in later life. The extent to which eventual adult ability can be predicted depends on the age of testing. At the age of 2 years the prediction of adult IQ is extremely inaccurate, while test scores

Table 5.3 Correlation of later IQ with earlier score

Age at initial test (years)	Age at later retest (years)			
	7	10	14	18
2	0.46	0.37	0.28	0.31
7	—	0.77	0.75	0.71
10	—	—	0.86	0.73
14	—	—	—	0.76

From Jensen (1973).

obtained on a child of 7 years are correlated with eventual adult IQ quite highly (see Table 5.3).

The effects of ageing are not identical for different types of ability. Those that depend more on educational attainment, such as verbal knowledge, tend to go on increasing until fairly late in life, while others that depend on mental speed and power, such as reasoning, peak earlier and decline more rapidly (see Fig. 5.2) The age-related decline is most clear when a task demands new learning or new associations within existing knowledge. Since the deficit can be minimised by slow presentation and the use of familiar material, it is possible to reduce the confusion often experienced by the elderly if information is provided in this way.

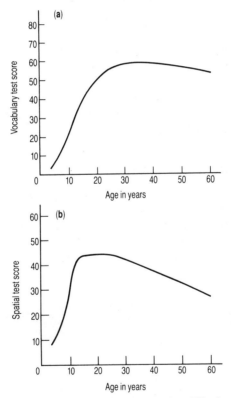

Fig. 5.2 Changes in (a) verbal and (b) spatial reasoning ability levels from age 10 to 60 years. The average score (50th percentile) declines slower for verbal than spatial reasoning (Reprinted with permission. From J. C. Raven, 'The comparative assessment of intellectual ability', British Journal of Psychology, 39, 1948, pp. 12–19.).

Specific abilities and intelligence

Intelligence is not a simple or unitary function of any one brain process, but an arbitrary (albeit useful) composite of different abilities. However, all mental abilities tend to be correlated with each other to some extent, so that people high on one tend also to be high on others. IQ tests are constructed precisely in order to measure this common general factor, and thus ignore individual patterns of ability. None the less, it is important to remember that an IQ score is a composite of several separate abilities such as verbal comprehension and fluency, ability with numbers, manipulation of objects in space, perceptual speed, memory, and reasoning, all involving different brain systems.

Localised brain damage will thus often disrupt some abilities more than others, so that change in the pattern of abilities is often a better guide to the nature of neurological damage than IQ scores alone.

PERSONALITY TRAITS

From shortly after birth, infants differ in many characteristics of behaviour, including activity level and emotional reactions to changes in their environment. Thus one child may be active and emotionally responsive to different people, while another might be quieter and react much less. These differences appear to be characteristic of particular children, and they also tend to persist: in one follow-up study they were still detectable 14 years later. Frequent displays of negative emotion in an infant tend to predict behaviour problems in later childhood.

Eysenck's personality dimensions

Consistency of a similar type emerges from the analysis of self-reported behaviour and preferences in adults. Work by Hans Eysenck (an eminent British psychologist) has shown that answers to questionnaire items concerned with preference for frequent social contact tend to form a characteristic pattern, indicating that sociability may be a specific trait that people possess to a greater or lesser degree. Since sociability tends to be associated with other traits, such as how lively, active, impulsive or excitable people report themselves to be, Eysenck prefers to describe them all as forming one general trait, known as *extraversion/introversion*.

Questionnaires measuring proneness to develop negative emotions such as anxiety and depression also intercorrelate, and are thus said to form another general trait called *emotionality or neuroticism*. These two general traits (extraversion and neuroticism) are relatively independent of one another (they do not intercorrelate), so that people can be highly extraverted and simultaneously either highly emotional, or extremely placid. Some psychologists, such as Cattell in the USA, feel that it is more useful to use tests that measure specific traits (e.g. outgoing, assertive, venturesome, etc.), which give a more detailed picture of individual personality, rather than averaging them to give a single extraversion score. However, there is considerable disagreement about the exact identity of some of these specific traits or how stable they are over time, whereas there is general agreement on the existence of the two general traits. On the other hand, perhaps because they are so general, it is difficult to make very useful predictions about individual behaviour based only on degree of extraversion and emotionality.

Biological bases of personality

The persistence of characteristic behaviours from birth suggests that, like intelligence, personality traits have their bases in genetic endowment. Identical twins tend to have moderately similar extraversion and neuroticism scores (correlations about 0.5) irrespective of whether they are reared together or apart. Eysenck has suggested that genetically determined variations in reactivity of the limbic system in the brain may account for differences in level of neuroticism, while extraversion may depend on level of cortical arousal. For a given level of stimulation introverts are thought to be more cortically aroused than extraverts, and thus need less external stimulation to maintain an optimal state. A related theory is that introverts are more reactive to mild punishment, are more easily socially conditioned as a result, and thus tend to learn the rules of social behaviour more readily. Such theories may have implications for understanding behavioural problems and emotional disorders. A highly emotional introvert might perhaps be very vulnerable to negative learning experiences.

Personality and abnormal behaviour

As its name implies, neuroticism (emotionality) is related to the risk of developing emotional disorders such as the neuroses.

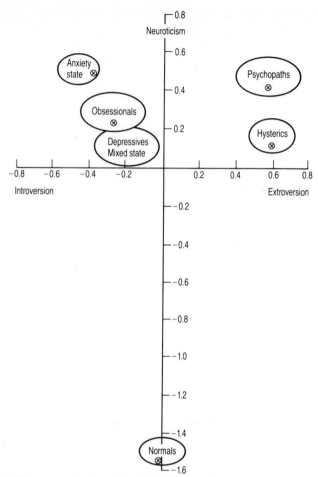

Fig. 5.3 Mean neuroticism and introversion/extraversion scores for groups with emotional or antisocial problems (From *A textbook of human psychology* by Eysenck and Wilson (1976), published by MTP Press Limited. Reprinted with permission.)

Patients suffering from clinical anxiety or depression generally score highly on neuroticism, and also tend to be introverted, that is, to have low extraversion scores. On the other hand, those with problems related to antisocial or aggressive behaviour tend to have high scores on both neuroticism and extraversion (see Fig. 5.3).

High emotionality would thus appear to be predictive of increased risk for developing behavioural or emotional problems, although the type of problem developed is influenced by introversion/extraversion. There is little evidence that these personality dimensions influence the exact form of emotional problem, such as types of phobia or obsessional disorder.

In non-psychiatric patients, high emotionality scores also predict reaction to medical treatment, such as slow or complicated recovery from surgery, or increased postsurgical pain. In one study, neuroticism was associated with postoperative chest complications; in another, the same score predicted length of stay in hospital (both correlations about 0.5). Extraversion seems more related to the way emotion is expressed, so that extraverted patients complain more vociferously about pain, and thus may receive more analgesics.

Psychological 'epidemics' of illness or physical symptoms also seem to be related to personality. In one such epidemic of fainting in a girls' school, one-third out of 500 pupils received in-patient care after symptoms of dizziness, paraesthesia and tetany, probably associated with overbreathing, swept through the school. Psychological testing revealed that those most affected were characterised by high extraversion and emotionality scores.

SOCIAL LEARNING AND PERSONALITY

Although studies of groups suggest that personality is generally predictive of the risk of developing social or emotional problems, personality tests are not very accurate at making predictions concerning single individuals. This may be partly due to the limited validity of self-report measures, but it also arises from the fact that much of human behaviour is inconsistent; it varies greatly according to context or setting condition. For example, it is not uncommon to find that a problem child is disobedient with his parents, but relatively well behaved at school (or vice versa). More experimental research in this area has confirmed that behaviour across different situations is sometimes consistent, but often is not. In one study, ratings of 'friendliness', for example, showed that agreement across different situations varied from low to moderate (correlations of 0.3 to 0.6). In the light of these findings it is perhaps surprising that we have such a strong impression that people are highly consistent in their behaviour. Several related reasons have been proposed, and some of these are listed below.

Stereotyping. We often assume that other people will behave in a way that is typical of the social, occupational, sexual or racial groups to which they happen to belong. Such expectations distort perception because we notice and remember conformity with stereotypes, while discarding inconsistencies as exceptional.

Attribution. Research has shown that we tend to attribute more of our own behaviour to external circumstances, while that of others is attributed to internal causes such as personality. For example, smokers commonly believe that they fail to give up smoking because of external pressures, while others attribute the same behaviour to lack of will-power.

Situational Control. One reason that we underestimate the influence of external circumstances in others is that the effect of factors such as social reinforcement may not be at all obvious to an observer who sees another person in only one setting. In the earlier example of a child judged disobedient if observed at home, but well behaved at school, the different degrees of situational control exerted in the two environments provides a more satisfactory explanation than does personality.

Social learning and clinical problems

Direct observation of the situational conditions that are associated with a particular behaviour can sometimes be useful in understanding clinical problems.

For example, the teachers of a 4-year-old child were concerned because she seemed so withdrawn and isolated in play-school. By recording her behaviour over several weeks they observed that her standing apart from other children tended to lead to adult attention, perhaps thereby reinforcing it. When the teachers changed their own behaviour to make adult attention dependent on her playing together with others, she rapidly became more involved with the other children in the class, and remained so at follow-up. Although such individual cases obviously require replication on a larger scale, they demonstrate how problems that are typically attributed to internal causes may also be related to environmental factors.

SEX DIFFERENCES AND SEXUAL BEHAVIOUR

Sexual differentiation begins with the development of the fetal gonad into testis or ovary under control of the sex chromosomes. Hormones produced by the developing gonads then determine the growth of different physical sexual characteristics, and also influence the development of the brain. As a result, male and female brains are already different at birth, and differences in the size of certain brain structures are detectable in adults.

Sex differences in behaviour

Sex differences in behaviour are the result of a complex interaction between biological development and early learning processes. Exposure of genetic females to excessive androgens in utero can result in behavioural as well as physical changes; girls may tend to engage in more active or aggressive play, for example. However, the adoption of sex-role behaviours is also strongly influenced by whether the child is reared as a boy or girl. In the condition known as *pseudohermaphrodism* a genetic male or female may develop inappropriate sex organs that require later surgical correction. Even if reared as a boy, a switch to the role of a girl (or vice versa) remains comparatively easy provided it is done before the age of 2 years. After that, the switch becomes progressively more difficult and children may have considerable problems in adapting to their 'true' sex role.

Sex differences in ability

Overall IQ levels do not differ between males and females, but this is the result of the deliberate selection of test material so as to balance out possible sex differences. There is good evidence that the sexes are characterised by different patterns of ability, rather than different overall levels. Girls tend to show earlier evidence of cerebral lateralisation (see Chapter 1) and tend to perform better in language tasks. Boys tend to be ahead in the ability to manipulate objects mentally in space, and also show more extreme scores at both the upper and lower ends of the ability spectrum. Despite this, the ranges of abilities overlap completely, and the small differences that do exist may well be amplified by social expectations.

Human sexual behaviour

Observation of the behaviour of children has shown that occasional genital self-stimulation may occur within the first year of life. If this continues, parental disapproval usually leads to concealment, so that later incidence is uncertain, although masturbation and related sex play is common in the years leading up to puberty. In adults, surveys suggest that more than 90% of men and about 60% of women have masturbated to orgasm, although such survey data may well be of limited validity. Current data suggest that more

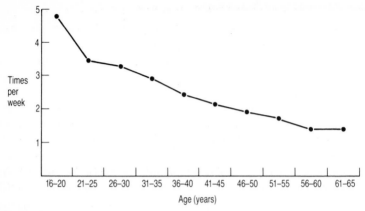

Fig. 5.4 Reported frequency of sexual intercourse by age (from Gebhard & Johnson 1979).

than 60% of the UK population have experienced sexual intercourse by the age of 18, and this proportion may well be increasing. Frequency of intercourse and other sexual activity in adults tends to reduce with age, from a weekly frequency of about four at the age of 20 years to about one at 65, depending on health and marital status (see Fig. 5.4)

The common stereotype of aggressive male and passive female sexuality has parallels in animal behaviour, but isolated human cultures with sex-role reversal in this respect have been described, suggesting that such differences are not fixed biologically. Physical and other attributes that are considered attractive in the opposite sex also vary with fashion and individual taste, again suggesting that learning may have a role. Although there is no evidence that sexual enjoyment differs much between the sexes, some data suggests that men are more rapidly aroused, especially by visual stimulation or fantasy, and that women respond more to other qualities in a relationship.

Sexual deviation

Deviance is a term used to describe behaviour that goes against current social norms. However, some sexual acts seen as deviant in a culture may be simultaneously normal in statistical terms (for example, oral–genital contact). Less common forms of deviance arise from changes in *sexual orientation*. Sexual interest may be directed away from the opposite sex, or exclusively towards one specific attribute or act. Illegal sexual behaviours, such as rape, incest, exhibitionism and paedophilia are also deviations, but will not be covered here.

Homosexuality

The most frequent variation of sexual orientation in both sexes is that of homosexuality. In one representative study, at least one homosexual experience was reported by about 30% of men, although only half of these experiences were after the age of 15 years, and only 3% of the sample were exclusively homosexual, with another 3% being bisexual. Corresponding figures for women are about half of those for men.

These figures demonstrate that homosexual behaviour is widespread, but that most of the individuals involved are not exclusively, or even predominantly, homosexual. Even exclusive homosexuals do not usually cross-dress or adopt the role behaviour of the opposite sex; nor are they physically or biologically distinguishable from heterosexuals. The incidence of emotional problems is often found to be relatively high, but this may be at least partly due to negative social discrimination. Permanent relationships certainly occur among homosexuals, although more commonly in women, with promiscuity being greater among men. It remains quite unclear whether homosexual behaviour is learned or results from biological variations (or both), but it is no longer regarded or treated as a disease.

Other sexual orientations

Most other sexual deviations are found almost entirely among men, although sadomasochistic behaviour can involve both sexes. Mild sadomasochism overlaps with normal behaviour but can develop into more specific and extreme forms such as whipping or bondage, sometimes combined with fetishism. Fetishism is an exclusive interest in specific objects such as female underwear, rubber garments, etc., which surprisingly can begin as early as 4 years of age, and nearly always before 20. Experimental studies have shown that sexual responses to common fetish objects can be conditioned by pairing them with sexual arousal induced in other ways.

Transvestites — men who are aroused by dressing in female clothes — should be distinguished from transsexuals of both sexes, who cross-dress because they regard themselves as being really a member of the opposite sex and thus may seek surgical 'correction'. The incidence and cause of these orientations are unknown, although again an early age of onset is commonly seen. Male transvestite behaviour often develops from early experiences of masturbating while cross-dressing, and can be treated by pairing cross-dressing with aversive stimuli. Unlike transvestism, transsexualism is very difficult to modify, so that permanent adoption of the cross-sex role together with surgical reconstruction may be appropriate.

Despite a lack of knowledge concerning the causes of sexual deviance, the wide range of sexual behaviour observed shows that, although sexual drive is biologically determined, learning or other environmental factors may cause it to be channelled in a variety of directions.

FURTHER READING

Bancroft J 1983 Human sexuality and its problems. Churchill Livingstone, Edinburgh
Pervin L 1984 Personality: theory and research (4th edn). Wiley, New York
Vernon P 1979 Intelligence: heredity and environment. W H Freeman, San Francisco

STUDY QUESTIONS

1. What is meant by 'reliability' and 'validity' of a personality test?
2. Assuming that a reliable and valid test has been used, what could be said of an individual with an IQ score of 70?
3. Describe the personality traits of extraversion and neuroticism, and their implications for emotional disturbance.
4. What factors other than personality traits influence differences in behaviour, and why are these factors often underestimated?
5. Do boys and girls differ consistently from each other in their abilities or personality?
6. What are the common forms of sexual deviation?

6

Emotion and stress

THE NATURE OF EMOTION

Emotion is a complex phenomenon since it has several distinct components that may sometimes change independently of one another.

(a) *Subjective feeling or affect.* In everyday language, emotion is typically used to describe moods such as joy, sadness and anger. These feelings cannot be measured directly, but only through verbal or written reports. Frequently, visual rating scales are used, on which subjects are asked to rate their emotions by marking a point on a line ranging from (for example) 'none' to 'extreme'.

(b) *Emotional behaviours.* These can in turn be divided into expressive reactions such as crying, laughing, smiling and emotion-related activities. The latter are frequently acquired through experience, and include complex sequences such as fighting or fearful avoidance.

(c) *Peripheral physiological reactions.* These are largely mediated through stimulation of the sympathetic branch of the autonomic nervous system, and include increases in heart rate, sweat gland activity and other parameters.

The components of emotion may respond in concert, as in some fearful situations when subjective ratings have been shown to covary with autonomic responses (see Fig. 6.1). Unfortunately, inconsistent patterns of response are also observed, and these add to the complexity of studying emotion. For example, someone who is anxious about enclosed spaces may avoid using a lift in a tall building (fear-related avoidance behaviour), but will not show any signs of subjective distress or autonomic activation. An expressive behaviour such as crying may be a sign of sadness or else of joy. Some words describing emotion may relate to particular patterns of response: 'courage', for instance, may indicate subjective fear and autonomic activation in the absence of avoidance behaviour.

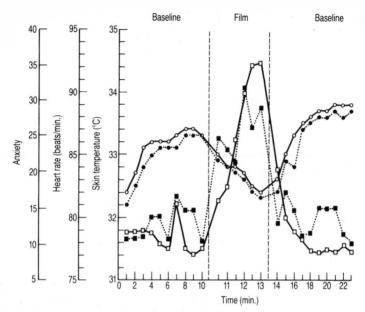

Fig. 6.1 The relationship between self-reported anxiety (□——————□) and the autonomic measures heart rate (■----■), right (○————○) and left (●-----●) hand temperature, recorded while volunteers watch a disturbing film. Hand temperature is used as a measure of vasconstriction in the skin. There is a close relationship between increases in anxiety and heart rate during the film, while blood flow in the skin is reduced (from Thayer et al 1984).

The basic components of an emotional response are illustrated schematically in Figure 6.2, and are explained in more detail below.

Emotion and the brain

The most important region of the brain concerned with emotion is the limbic system, including the amygdala, hippocampus, septal area and cingulate gyrus, together with the hypothamalus. Lesion studies carried out by physiologists such as Sherrington & Bard indicated that emotional behaviours persisted in animals following ablation of the neocortex. Cats left with only the hypothalamus and lower brain structures show 'sham rage', a hypersensitive generalised emotional response to normally unprovocative stimuli. More recent stimulation and lesion studies indicate that aggressive behaviour and fear may be either enhanced or reduced depending on the specific site in the brain that is affected. It is possible that specific

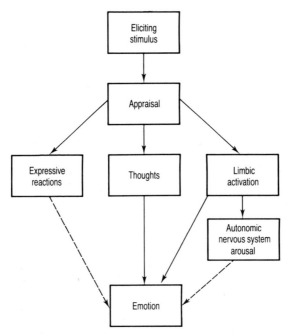

Fig. 6.2 A schematic model of emotional processes.

subcortical circuits mediate different emotions. Furthermore, the effects of lesions may also depend on the external environment. The American psychologist Karl Pribram found that identical bilateral lesions of the amygdala in monkeys either increased or decreased aggressive behaviour in monkeys, depending on whether or not the animals were placed within a competitive environment. This suggests that cognitive processes taking place within the neocortex exert a strong influence over emotional activity.

The surgical control of aggression

Reports from animal experiments showing placidity following ablation of the medial temporal lobe (including the amygdala and hippocampus), coupled with cases in which multiple murderers were found to have tumours in the limbic system, led to the use of 'psychosurgery' in the middle of the century. This involved lesioning limbic structures using electrical or chemical techniques in an effort to control disruptive behaviour. However, this treatment was evaluated poorly and in a biased fashion. The irreversible nature of the procedure and the possibility of serious intellectual impairment has led to its restriction to a few centres of enthusiasm. The development of more effective psychotropic medication has further reduced the use of psychosurgery, although many people also have misgivings about the dangers of pharmacological control.

Cognitive processes in emotion

As can be seen in Figure 6.2, stimuli that elicit emotion are first subjected to an appraisal process. The initial appraisal is a rapid, largely unconscious perceptual process, and we are normally only aware of the resulting emotional state. The main cognitive processes concern the evaluation and interpretation of the situation as funny, dangerous, etc. We differ in our interpretation of stimuli according to previous experiences, values and motivational state. Thus one person may think an obscene joke is funny, while another will be disgusted. There is some evidence that the two cerebral hemispheres are involved in the processing of emotion to varying degrees, with suggestions either that the right hemisphere is specialised for emotion, or that positive emotions are processed in the left, and negative emotions in the right hemisphere. However, the nature of this difference is not yet clear.

Autonomic activity in emotion

Many of the autonomic responses that occur in emotional states can be measured unobtrusively using *psychophysiological* techniques. They include increases in heart rate and blood pressure, decreases in blood flow to the skin (resulting in the characteristic pallor of people experiencing extreme emotion), disturbances in breathing pattern and increases in palmar sweat gland activity (typically measured in terms of skin conductance). Striate musculature is also affected, leading to increases in muscle tension and trembling, while increases in high frequency (β) activity may be seen in the EEG. These responses are components of the emergency 'fight or flight' response, a phylogenetically primitive reaction pattern in which the organism is rapidly prepared for physical work.

There has been much debate about whether different emotions are characterised by varying patterns of peripheral physiological response. Although some experiments have shown slight differences, most suggest that the activation associated with emotion is non-specific; physiological responses vary with the intensity of emotion, but not its quality. Recent experiments also suggest that different forms of emotional expression elicit varying physiological responses. Some researchers argue that emotionally expressive behaviours may alter subjective experience — when you frown you feel less positive — hence the dotted line connecting expressive reactions with emotion in Figure 6.2.

Perceived arousal and emotional state

Physiological activation may be not only a product of emotion, but may also affect the intensity of the subjective experience. When peripheral activation is induced through injection of adrenaline, people seldom report genuine emotions, but rather say that they feel 'as if' they are emotionally aroused. In an influential set of experiments, the American psychologist Stanley Schachter argued that physiological arousal may lead to increased feelings of emotion provided that it is experienced in an appropriate context. Subjects were administered with placebo or adrenaline in a disguised form. Subsequently, the subject entered a room where another person was displaying either euphoric behaviour (laughing and dancing), or else behaved in an insulting and anger-provoking fashion. It was found that little mood change followed placebo administration, regardless of social context. But in the adrenaline condition, subjects reported either amusement or anger, depending on the situation in which they found themselves. Schachter suggested that these subjects had no ready explanation of their aroused state, so they interpreted it in terms of their social environment.

Schachter's studies are open to numerous methodological criticisms, and not all of his results have been replicated in other experiments. However, it is still true that, under certain conditions, perception of physiological arousal affects emotional experience. For example, when people have been aroused physiologically by some neutral activity (such as physical exercise) their response to emotional stimuli may be enhanced. Sexual arousal may be more intense after a person has just escaped from danger. This pattern can also be significant in some emotional disorders. An anxious patient might become aroused through physical exertion and then falsely interpret his or her somatic state (palpitations, breathlessness, etc.) as symptoms of an impending panic attack.

STRESS AND COPING

Psychological stress has been defined as a set of stimuli (calamitous events, particular work environments, etc.) or alternatively as a set of responses (the physiological and emotional adjustments that might take place in such circumstances). However, stress is probably best viewed as an interactive process which arises when the demands of the environment exceed the capacity and resources of the individual concerned. Thus a particular 'stressful' event (such as a deadline at work) will be perceived differently depending on the psychological resources available. One person might perceive the deadline as a serious threat, taxing his or her capacity to the utmost, while another might perceive it as a positive challenge that can be overcome given hard work and organisation.

The notion of stress is closely bound up with psychological coping. Psychological coping is the process of managing stress, and its function is to enable a person to tolerate or adjust to adverse events, and to maintain emotional and physiological equilibrium. According to Richard Lazarus, there are two stages to coping. In primary appraisal, the environment is evaluated for its potential threat and for the possible harm or challenges it holds. Experiments have shown that the autonomic responses to potentially distressing stimuli can be modified by the way in which events are

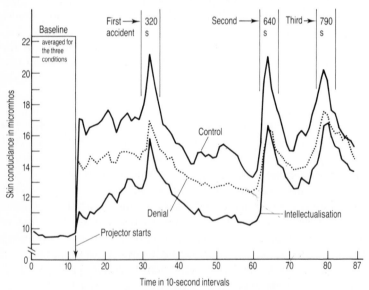

Fig. 6.3 Skin conductance in three groups of volunteers watching a film that included three serious industrial accidents. The groups are given different instructions about how to appraise the film (Reprinted with permission. From: Richard S. Lazarus, Edward M. Opton, Jr., Markello S, Nomikos and Neil O. Rankin, 'The principle of short-circuiting of threat: further evidence,' in Journal of Personality 33:4, pg. 628. Copyright © 1965 Duke University Press.)

appraised cognitively. Figure 6.3 shows the results of an experiment in which volunteers watched a film containing gory accidents. Autonomic reactions were reduced when subjects were instructed to intellectualise the experience, focusing their attention away from the emotional content of the film in order to concentrate on technical aspects of the production, or else were reminded that the incidents were staged and not real (denial). These strategies may exert their effects by distracting people from the threatening components of the experience.

Once a stimulus has been perceived as stressful, the second stage of coping occurs, in which the question 'What can I do about it?' is addressed. Physical, emotional and social resources are evaluated in relation to the demands of the occasion. Coping responses themselves also take two general forms: direct actions or *problem-focused coping*, which involve attempts to alter the situation — an example might be escaping from the situation or controlling the source of stress; and *emotion-focused coping*, in which attempts are made to modify the distress associated with the experience. Such palliative actions may range from taking drugs or alcohol to prayer or re-interpreting the situation mentally. In one study, emotion-focused coping was assessed in helicopter ambulance crews flying into dangerous battlegrounds during the Vietnam war. A wide variety of coping strategies were observed, including denial, attempts at distraction, fatalism, mental dissociation from the situation and intellectualisation of the chances of survival.

Stress and its management

Patients are increasingly turning to general practitioners to help them cope with a range of stressful experiences, from important examinations to redundancy and marital breakdown. Since the 1970s, benzodiazepines such as diazepam have become the most commonly prescribed drugs, and have been taken by 10–20% of the population. Although tranquillisers are effective in the short term, there is increasing concern about their use in the management of stress-related problems. Many patients become reliant on them, and pharmacological dependence can develop, with a withdrawal syndrome that includes symptoms of anxiety and perceptual disturbances which emerge when the drug is stopped.

Clinical psychologists have developed non-pharmacological stress management techniques that provide useful alternatives. These methods include helping people to organise their time effectively so that they do not feel overwhelmed by demands on

them, training in relaxation as a coping strategy, and training
people to re-appraise the environment more adaptively, so that
events are perceived in a less threatening fashion.

Physiological stress responses

Physiological stress reactions include the adjustments described
earlier that accompany emotional behaviour, but usually involve
more extensive changes in activity. These responses are summarised in Table 6.1, and are primarily mediated through two
pathways:

(a) The *sympathetic nervous system* acts directly on target organs,
    and also indirectly through catecholamine release from the
    adrenal medulla. Effects include the redistribution of blood to
    the skeletal muscle beds at the expense of the skin and viscera,
    and increases in heart rate and cardiac contractility. The cat-
    echolamines enhance platelet aggregation, speeding blood co-
    agulation and clot formation. Other effects include pilo-erection,
    sweating and reduced salivation.

(b) The *hypothalamic pituitary–adrenocortical axis* regulates a
    number of hormones. The glucocorticoids (cortisol in humans
    and corticosterone in animals) are particularly important in
    stress reactions. In conjunction with catecholamines, they
    promote the mobilisation of stored fats and their conversion to
    free fatty acids and triglycerides. Inflammatory reactions are
    reduced by the action of corticosteroids, so immunological
    response may also be altered.

This response pattern is integrated in the hypothalamus, and is
a vital part of the organism's defence system. However, the
biological function of the glucocorticoid response is difficult to
understand, since suppression of inflamatory processes may
increase vulnerability. It is possible that the glucocorticoid changes
have a regulatory purpose, preventing overshoot of other defence
mechanisms. The pattern was studied intensively by Hans Selye
who coined the term *general adaptation syndrome* to describe the way
in which physiological stress responses affect the resistance to
stimulation from the environment. Selye's original concept is now
disputed, since physiological reactions are not generalised or non-
specific, but selective. The pituitary–adrenocortical axis is stimulated more during exposure to aversive events that are beyond the
individual's control and must be tolerated passively. The sympathetic nervous system, on the other hand, tends to respond to active

Table 6.1 Physiological stress responses

Effector pathways

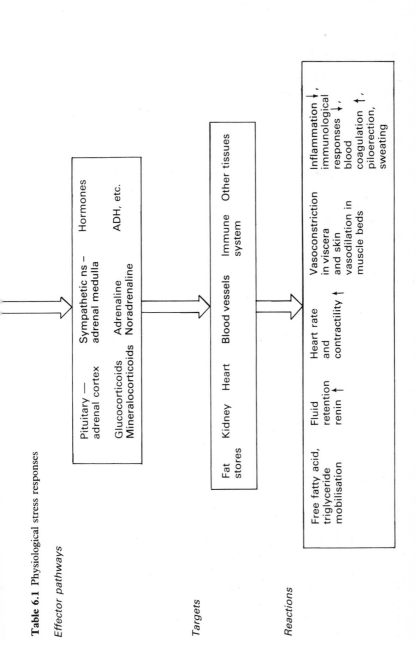

		Pituitary — adrenal cortex	Sympathetic ns – adrenal medulla	Hormones
		Glucocorticoids Mineralocorticoids	Adrenaline Noradrenaline	ADH, etc.

Targets

Fat stores	Kidney	Heart	Blood vessels	Immune system	Other tissues

Reactions

Free fatty acid, triglyceride mobilisation	Fluid retention renin ↑	Heart rate and contractility ↑	Vasoconstriction in viscera and skin vasodilation in muscle beds	Inflammation ↓, immunological responses ↓, blood coagulation ↑, piloerection, sweating

challenge (see below). These physiological disturbances may lead to heightened risk of disease (see Chapter 7).

Influence of novelty and predictability

When animals are exposed to unfamiliar and potentially dangerous conditions, they show large neuroendocrine reactions. The concentration of corticosteroids and catecholamines in the blood increases many times over when animals are first introduced to an experimental apparatus, or even when their cage doors are opened. Similar effects in humans have been seen during the training of parachutists, divers and lifeboat crew. However, these responses diminish as the circumstances become more familiar and mastery of the threatening conditions is acquired. Figure 6.4 illustrates the autonomic reactions of novice and skilled parachutists during the sequence of events leading to a jump. Activation (indexed by heart rate, breathing rate and skin conductance) increases in the early

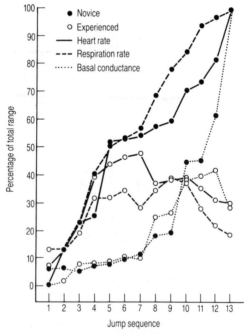

Fig. 6.4 Heart rate, respiration rate and basal skin conductance, expressed in percentage scores of total range, for novice and experienced parachutists throughout a sequence of events leading up to a jump (From Fenz in: Sarason/Spielberger (1972) 'Stress and anxiety' Vol. 2, p 320, figure 15–16, published by Hemisphere Publishing Corporation. Reprinted with permission.)

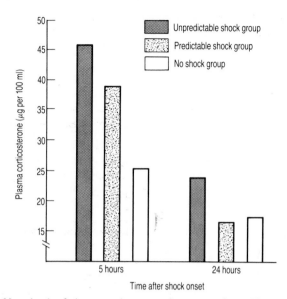

Fig. 6.5 Mean levels of plasma corticosterone for groups of rats (N = 10 per group) sacrificed at different stages of the predictable/unpredictable shock experiment (From Weiss (1970), Psychosomatic Medicine (32). Reprinted with permission.)

stages in both groups. But after aircraft warm-up and take-off (stages 6–9), the responses of the experienced parachutists flatten out. In contrast, novices show progressive increases in activation throughout the sequence.

Predictability is another factor that modulates stress responses. The combined effect of novelty and predictability on pituitary–adrenocortical activation in rats is shown in Figure 6.5. One group was given a series of unpredictable electric shocks through electrodes attached to their tails. Precisely the same sequence was used a group given predictable shock, but in this case each shock was preceded by a 10-second tone. The third group acted as a no-shock control. The reduction in corticosterone responses between 5 and 24 hours shows the effects of novelty wearing off. Over and above this, steroid responses were consistently greater in the unpredictable than in predictable shock conditions, even though the physical trauma (duration and intensity of painful stimulation) was identical.

Experimental studies in humans have compared behavioural performance on clerical tasks in subjects exposed to distracting noise (a medley of office sounds, traffic noise, etc.) presented either in a regular pattern or unpredictably. It has been found that even after the noise sequence had stopped, task performance was poorer in the people who have experienced unpredictable bursts of noise, with more errors and reduced work efficiency.

Stress in surgical patients

Entering hospital for surgery fulfils all the criteria for being highly stressful. Not only may the patient have a dangerous, possibly life-threatening disorder, but surgery itself is a novel, unpredictable and often painful experience. Patients are removed from their everyday environment into an unfamiliar place where their fate is uncertain. Studies of patients admitted for surgery show high levels of anxiety and depression around the operative period, together with autonomic and neuroendocrine activation. Distress may remain high or even increase in the immediate postoperative period; anxiety does not decline as soon as the operation is over, as many surgeons expect. Individual patients do, however, vary enormously in the severity of these reactions, probably depending on coping strategy or personality differences (see Chapter 5), and there is a strong tendency for more distressed patients to recover more slowly from surgery.

Control and coping

The psychophysiological responses to noxious stimuli also vary with the degree of control that can be exercised. Everyday experience tells us that when we have personal control over unpleasant conditions we will tolerate more. Enthusiastic hikers may be very happy to trudge through wet and muddy fields for their own enjoyment, but would be upset if they were made to do the same things by someone else. In laboratory experiments, subjects will tolerate greater amounts of painful stimulation if they believe that they have personal control. Neuroendocrine responses follow the same pattern. In one study, plasma cortisol responses were measured in monkeys exposed to high intensity noise. One group was able to switch the sound off by pressing a lever, while in the second group the sound was switched off at the same time by the experimenter. Cortisol responses were diminished in the group with control, even though the duration and intensity of noise was identical in the two cases. The effects of control may extend beyond conditions in which objective control is achieved to the sense of control or mastery over the environment. This cognitive control is an important form of coping response.

Active behavioural coping

The effects of control are not always beneficial. If control over the source of stress is difficult to achieve, reactions may be heightened. Table 6.2 summarises the results of a study in which volunteers were threatened with loud noise bursts during performance of easy or difficult puzzles. Half the subjects were told that noise would be random (no control), while the remainder were told that noise depended on level of performance of the task (control). Although both groups in fact heard identical amounts of noise, the blood-pressure reactions were greatest among subjects who believed they could exert control by solving difficult puzzles. Their responses were greater than those in the uncontrollable condition or in the easy-task group.

Table 6.2 Blood pressure reactions during task performance under threat of aversive noise (from Manuck et al, 1978)

Experimental groups ($n = 11$ per group)	Average blood pressure changes from baseline (mmHg)	
	Systolic	Diastolic
Control — task difficult	23.4	7.7
No control — task difficult	12.1	3.9
Control — task easy	9.4	3.6
No control — task easy	13.8	3.9

People exposed to challenging environments who exert considerable efforts in their attempts to maintain control are said to exhibit active behavioural coping. Active behavioural coping is associated with stimulation of the cardiac sympathetic nerves and other pathways mediated by beta adrenoceptors, and is accompanied by increases in heart rate, blood-pressure and myocardial contractility. This pattern may be significant in the development of cardio-vascular disorders (see Chapter 7).

Psychological preparation for surgery

In 1964, a study was published by Egbert and co-workers in

which patients undergoing abdominal surgery were randomly allocated to special care and control groups. Patients in the special care group were given detailed information before surgery concerning the procedure and its effects, together with advice on how to cope with it. This group required fewer postoperative narcotics throughout the recovery period, and were also discharged an average of 2.7 days before controls, despite the medical and surgical staff being blind to treatment conditions. Since then, a large number of studies have been carried out into the psychological preparation for surgery, and patients are routinely given much more information about their surgery than in the past.

Several different types of psychological preparation are used, including practical information about the procedure, information about the sensations likely to be experienced, and coping instructions. The coping methods include relaxation training and cognitive coping techniques. In the latter, patients are shown that they can change the way they view events by concentrating on the more positive aspects. For example, patients' worries about the anaesthetic might be countered by the thought that 'Many thousands of people have general anaesthesia every year; they do well and so will I'. Experimental comparisons suggest that giving procedural information is less effective than the provision of coping strategies. Effects are seen in terms of postoperative mood and pain, medication requirements and other variables.

A useful method of preparing children for surgery is based on the principle of modelling (see Chapter 3). Films are prepared in which the experiences of a child undergoing surgery are followed from admission to hospital through to discharge. The method alleviates children's distress by showing them what is going to happen and what they are likely to feel. The model in the film does not pretend that the procedure is harmless and pain free, but voices his or her fears and worries, so that the real patients can identify with them.

STRESS AND LIFE EVENTS

One of the major problems in studying stress in medical disorders is quantification. Since individuals differ so much in their reactions, how do we measure the amount of potential harm that is present in any set of circumstances? One of the most important techniques for overcoming this problem is to measure *life events*. A life event is a change in a person's social or physical environment that can be measured objectively. Life events occur in many areas of life, including work, family and relationships with other people.

Table 6.3 An extract from a life event inventory, showing the type of occurrence that is assessed

Work:
— Change to new job
— Promotion at work
— Made redundant or fired
— Spouse/partner changed to a new job
— Unemployed for a month or more

Failing health:
— Death of a spouse/partner
— Serious physical or emotional illness of close family member (parent, brother, sister, children)
— Death of a close friend

Marital and social:
— Separation from spouse/partner
— Divorce
— New person (e.g. tenant or relative) living in the household
— Marital problems of a close family member (e.g. parent, child, brother or sister)

Financial and legal:
— Major financial difficulties, much worse than usual (e.g. very heavy debts or expenses)
— Major improvement in finances (unexpected gift, rent or tax rebate, inheritance, etc.)
— Court appearance
— Close friend sentenced to jail/borstal

Lists are drawn up of life changes, including such items as marriage, birth of a child, changing jobs or moving house, and subjects are asked whether these have occurred over a defined time. Table 6.3 shows a sample of life events. Life events are used to study the effects of personal experience on health by measuring their occurrence in people with a particular disorder. Since everyone experiences some events, the rates of life events in illness groups must always be compared against that of controls.

The two principal methods of assessing life events are by questionnaire and interview. Questionnaires include the Schedule of Recent Events, and the Social Re-adjustment Rating Scale, in which people tick off the events they have experienced from a long list. Standardised interviews have been developed by Brown (a sociologist) and by Paykel (a psychiatrist) in which the impact of each event is explored in depth. There are several problems in recording life events. The first is *recall*. It is easy to forget what has happened, or precisely when a particular event took place. Sometime patients exaggerate the importance of an event because an illness developed after it. A second problem is *independence*.

Although some stressful events may cause disease, disease can also cause events; for example, a person may lose their job through ill health. These problems can better be resolved using interview techniques than pencil-and-paper questionnaires, so that the circumstances surrounding the event can be evaluated in detail.

The third problem is the measurement of *severity*. The death of a spouse and a child leaving home to live elsewhere are both life events, but they are unlikely to be equally distressing. In some studies, events are weighted according to a pre-arranged scoring system (e.g. marital separation has a score of 65, and end of formal schooling 26) and are then summed. This technique assumes events are additive, and that the same event is of equal importance for different people. This may not be true — divorce may be a major crisis for some individuals, but a blessing for others. Alternative methods classify events according to whether or not they are severely threatening, or separate them into broad types (losses, threats, exits from the individual's social world, etc.).

The impact of life events is also influenced by a number of *moderating factors*, the most important of which are social supports and the availability of confidantes with which to share the burden. The influence of life events on emotional and medical disorders is covered in greater detail in Chapters 7 and 9.

FURTHER READING

Feuerstein M, Labbé E E, Kuczmierczyk A R 1985 Health psychology: a psychobiological perspective. Plenum Press, New York
Goldberger L, Breznitz S (eds) 1982 Handbook of stress. Free Press, New York
Levitt R A 1981 Physiological psychology. Holt, Rinehart and Winston, New York

STUDY QUESTIONS

1. Can different emotions be distinguished at the physiological level?
2. What brain mechanisms are involved in emotion?
3. What is meant by psychological coping?
4. What factors influence the intensity of stress responses?
5. How can distress in hospital patients be alleviated?
6. What problems arise in the measurement of life events?

7

Psychological factors in medical disorders

STRESS AND DISEASE

The role of psychological factors in medical disorders has been studied for many years, and forms the basis of psychosomatic medicine. Early research stemmed from the theory that psychological or emotional conflicts might predispose towards specific diseases. For example, the suppression of hostile feelings was thought to be linked with essential hypertension, and dependency conflicts with bronchial asthma. These studies suffered from many methodological problems and had little impact on our understanding of disease processes. Current research is more concerned with the influence of the physical and psychosocial environment on physiological systems, and their interaction with individual disease predispositions.

Several types of evidence contribute to theories that psychological factors and behavioural stress affect medical disorders.

(a) Short term experiments with humans demonstrate that autonomic and endocrine responses occur during behavioural stress in the laboratory.

(b) Clinical and epidemiological studies suggest that people exposed to intense psychosocial stress are at high risk for illness.

(c) Experimental studies of animals show that disease can arise following prolonged behavioural stress under carefully regulated conditions in which confounding factors are controlled.

(d) Pathophysiological studies provide information about the pathways that mediate these effects. Abnormal activity in the autonomic nervous system and neuroendocrine pathways can promote a variety of diseases, including cardiovascular disorders (essential hypertension and ischaemic heart diseases), infection and malignancy.

In some cases, the link between psychosocial factors and illness

93

may be *chronic*, affecting the long term aetiology of the disorder. Other associations may be *acute*, triggering a clinical event such as myocardial infarction in a patient already seriously at risk. Behavioural factors may *initiate* the disease process, or else *exacerbate* existing pathology, for example by impairing the immune defence against infection.

Maladaptive physiological responses

The physiological stress responses outlined in Chapter 6 prepare the organism for vigorous activity. However, the same physiological reactions are also evoked when active behaviours such as fighting or escaping are not appropriate. In our everyday lives, many of the harassing or distressing conditions we encounter cannot be overcome by physical action. It is thought that physiological stress responses may be dangerous if they are not dispersed or diffused by some sort of activity. Thus high levels of circulating catecholamines may influence cardiac muscle and vascular beds, while high concentrations of free fatty acids may eventually increase the levels of cholesterol in the plasma. The suppression of immune function initiated by high levels of circulating corticosteroids increases vulnerability to infection and other disorders.

It is therefore possible that repeated elicitation of physiological stress responses increase the risk of disease. The link is difficult to study in humans, because effects may take many years to develop, but acute responses are regularly seen. Anticipation of academic exams, interviews, conference presentations and important sporting occasions all involve activation of the sympathetic–catecholamine and adrenocortical systems. The long term links with disease have also been studied in animals. James Henry and his co-workers (1975) have carried out a series of studies of male mice weaned in isolation, and subsequently placed in competitive social colonies for varying periods of time. Figure 7.1 shows that increases in blood pressure occur even after a short time in the colony. This reaction is reversible if exposure to psychosocial competition is brief. However, hypertension becomes permanent with prolonged residence in the colony, while myocardial degeneration eventually develops. Other forms of organic pathology, including gastrointestinal and renal diseases and disturbances of male and female fertility, have also been observed in animals following behavioural stress.

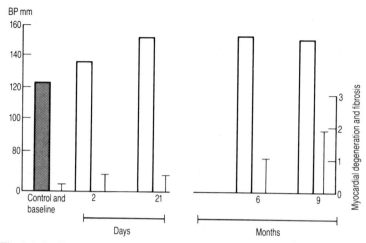

Fig. 7.1 Cardiovascular pathology in male mice following times in population cages. The open histograms indicate average systolic pressure while the black bars show the incidence of myocardial degeneration. The time-scale refers to the length of time for which previously isolated males were placed in population cages (i.e. between 2 days and 9 months). Blood pressure increases immediately, while the heart is damaged only after longer periods of stimulation (from Henry et al 1975).

Psychoimmunology

Research in recent years has shown that cell-mediated and humoral immune function can be influenced by psychological processes. Immune responses can be classically conditioned by pairing a neutral stimulus (CS) with a drug that produces immunosuppression (UCS). After only a single CS–UCS pairing, presentation of the CS can induce an immunosuppressive response (CR). The disturbances of immune function elicited by behavioural stress may also affect tumour growth. Figure 7.2 shows the results of a study in which mastocytoma cells were transplanted into mice that were then allocated to three groups. Two groups were administered a series of electric shocks over a single session. One of these could escape the shocks by moving to the opposite side of the cage (escapable shock group), while the second group could not escape (inescapable shock group). However, animals in the inescapable shock group were 'yoked' or matched to rats in the escapable shock group, so that the amount of shock received was identical. The only factor distinguishing these groups was therefore the controllability of the aversive experience. A third group acted as no-shock

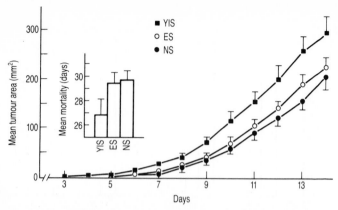

Fig. 7.2 Mean (±SE) tumour area over days, as well as mean day of mortality (inset) among mice that received escapable shock (ES), yoked inescapable shock (YIS) or no shock (NS) (From 'Stress and coping factors influence tumor growth', Sklar and Anisman, Vol. 205, pp 513–515, 3 August 1979. Copyright 1979 by AAAS.)

controls. It can be seen that tumour growth was more rapid in the inescapable shock group; these animals also succumbed more rapidly to the malignancy. The ability to control the stimulation in the escapable shock group was sufficient to eliminate the immuno-suppressive effect of the shock itself.

Acute reactions in humans

It was shown in Chapter 6 that performance of mentally challenging tasks provokes short term increases in blood-pressure, heart rate, catecholamines and other parameters in humans. These patterns may be part of the link between psychosocial stress and illness. When people with disorders such as essential hypertension and bronchial asthma are exposed to mentally taxing conditions in the laboratory, they show exaggerated reactivity in the physiological parameters relevant to their disorder (blood pressure for hypertensives, airways responses for asthmatics). In the case of essential hypertension, this is not simply a by-product of the disease state, since exaggerated reactivity is present in people who do not have hypertension but are nevertheless at high risk.

An example is shown in Figure 7.3, in which young adults with and without a parental history of hypertension were compared (it is known that hypertension carries a familial risk). Blood pressure and heart rate were recorded at rest and during performance of mental arithmetic problems. It can be seen that in the baseline

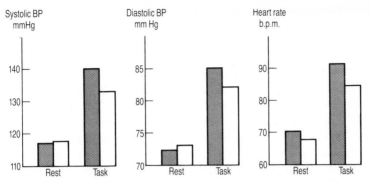

Fig. 7.3 Blood-pressure and heart rate at rest and during performance of mental arithmetic tasks in young men with (shaded bars) and without (open bars) a family history of hypertension (from Schulte et al 1981).

there are no differences between subjects with and without a positive family history. However, heightened blood pressure and heart rate responses to mental arithmetic are produced by those with a family history. This indicates that exaggerated behavioural stress responses are present before the disorder has developed. They may be partly responsible for putting the offspring of hypertensives at heightened risk.

METHODS OF STUDYING PSYCHOSOCIAL STRESS AND DISEASE

The experimental studies just described indicate that psychosocial factors can affect physiological disease processes, but do not demonstrate that they are actually significant in typical cases of illness. Clinical and epidemiological data help to establish this connection. One way of investigating such effects is to compare people of similar background and status who differ in having more or less 'stressful' occupations. Cobb & Rose have carried out studies with air-traffic controllers, since they have very demanding and involving jobs that carry heavy responsibilities. In comparisons with airport staff who work in a similar environment, the controllers have a higher incidence of hypertension, and also develop hypertension at an earlier age. Differences in the prevalence of peptic ulcer were found as well. Similar patterns have been seen with other occupations where a high work-rate is linked with comparatively little control over the pace and organisation of the work.

However, problems can arise in this sort of comparison. Jobs may differ not only in terms of psychosocial stress, but also in activities (e.g. exercise and the possibility of smoking during work) that themselves contribute to disease. Furthermore, people choose their own occupations, so it is possible that a selection factor operates; perhaps the factors leading people to choose a particular career are associated with risk of disease.

A second approach is to modify the psychosocial environment and record any changes in morbidity. An important study was carried out by Purcell to test the involvement of emotional factors in childhood bronchial asthma. For a 2-week experimental period the asthmatic children were separated from their parents and siblings. The families agreed to go away and stay in a hotel while patients were looked after by a substitute who maintained the family's eating, exercise and domestic routines as normal. Separation was carried out in this way so as to avoid changes in exposure to allergens and other factors that might influence asthma. It was found that during the separation period the asthmatic condition improved dramatically, only to deteriorate again when the families were reunited. This study indicates that, in some asthmatics, emotional factors modulate clinical state and the severity of symptoms.

Retrospective studies

A common method of assessing whether psychosocial factors are involved in disease aetiology is to examine people who suffer from a disorder, and to measure how they differ from healthy controls. This technique has been used to study personality and life stress in patients with cancer, ischaemic heart disease, ulcers and other complaints. It is then argued that these factors (e.g. increased neuroticism or difficulty in expressing emotions) were present before the disease developed, and may have been partly responsible for its progression. However, retrospective comparisons are confounded by:

(a) *Reporting bias.* Once someone knows they have a disorder, they may connect it with earlier 'stress' in their lives, exaggerating the pressures under which they were living before.

(b) *Changes with onset.* Personal characteristics may be altered as a result of the illness. For example, newly diagnosed cancer patients may undergo many psychological changes as they adjust to their new status. Responses to personality assessments may therefore be different before and after disease onset and diagnosis.

(c) *Selective survival.* In the case of serious diseases such as ischaemic heart disease, a proportion of people may die before they are tested psychologically. The psychological experience of people who survive may be different from that of early victims of the disease.

The life-event technique (see Chapter 6) has been used to circumvent some of these difficulties when it comes to measuring life experience.

Life events and moderating variables

When studying the effects of life events on health, a factor that must be taken into account is *illness behaviour*. A large number of cases of mild illness never come to the attention of medical services. People vary in the extent of their illness behaviour, or the amount they complain about ill health and seek attention for it. Some individuals are disturbed by apparently trivial problems, while others seem to undergo pain and discomfort without deciding to see a doctor. Illness behaviour is affected by many factors such as family habits, personality and living conditions. People who find their lives or work satisfying are less likely to complain of symptoms than the bored or unhappy. Nevertheless, life events have been linked with the actual experience of severe illness, as well as with complaint behaviour.

Effects of bereavement

Some of the most striking evidence comes from the study of bereaved people. The death of a spouse or close relative is an event of profound importance. Of course, the way individuals react may vary greatly according to the intimacy of the bond, but most people experience bereavement as highly distressing. In Figure 7.4 it can be seen that the experience of bereavement increased death rates among the bereaved themselves, in comparison with matched controls. The difference was greatest in the first few months following bereavement. In another survey, widowers over the age of 55 years were followed up over several years. Their mortality rate was more than 40% above that expected for a population of their age for the first 6 months following the death of their wives. It was found that cardiovascular disorders (myocardial infarction

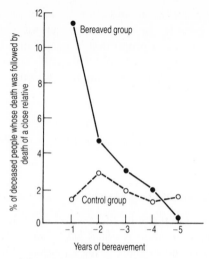

Fig. 7.4 Percentage of deceased people whose death was followed each year by the death of a close relative, as compared with a control cohort (from Rees & Lutkins 1967).

and stroke) were 60% higher than the base rate. Among younger groups deaths are rare, although greater numbers of the bereaved enter hospital over the first months following the loss. It is also possible that bereaved subjects are more susceptible to infection, since it has been shown that immunological function is significantly depressed in this group.

Other life events

Many studies have shown a raised incidence of life events in the period immediately preceding disease onset in conditions such as myocardial infarction, functional gastrointestinal disorders and appendicitis. Even in cases where the organic aetiology of the disorder is well understood, life events may increase the likelihood of illness. A longitudinal study of throat infections was carried out in a number of families, and throat swabs were regularly cultured for beta haemolytic streptococci. The incidence of positive streptococcal cultures was much higher than the rate of illness, so infection did not necessarily lead to symptoms. However, the acquisition of streptococci was more likely to lead to an overt illness if it was preceded by an acute life event.

Social support and social networks

Several factors may modify the consequences of a life event, and some of these are discussed in Chapter 9. In the case of medical disorders, the presence of a supportive social environment is important. Social supports are related to the extent of a person's social network — the number of relatives and friends with which they are in contact, and to whom they can turn for material and emotional aid in times of distress. The study of birth complications described on page 46 measured life events early in pregnancy. For women with low life-change scores, the presence of social supports made little difference to outcome. But among those with high life change, social supports exerted a critical mediating influence. The incidence of pregnancy and labour complications was 91% among women with high life-change and low social support scores, compared with 33.3% with similar life-change but strong social supports. It appeared that a supportive social network reduced the deleterious effects of life events on health. However, the relative contribution of social support and events is often difficult to tease out, since many life events (e.g. moving house, bereavement) simultaneously alter the person's social network.

Psychosocial factors and cancer

The experimental data outlined in Figure 7.2 suggests that psychosocial factors can influence the progression of cancer, even though they do not cause the disease. Numerous investigations have been conducted on the psychosocial and personality characteristics related to cancer, but often the methods used have been unsatisfactory and results inconsistent. There is, however, good evidence that once cancer has been diagnosed, psychological reactions have an impact on the course of the disease (as in the laboratory studies of animals). Greer and co-workers in London have assessed the psychological responses of women with breast cancer 3 months after mastectomy. Five years later, recurrence-free survival was more common among patients who had coped with the diagnosis by denial, or showed 'fighting spirit' in response to the disease. In contrast, patients who had responded with stoic acceptance or feelings of helplessness and hopelessness were less likely to have survived 5 years. These findings were not due to initial biological differences or tumour mass. They suggest that the way people cope with the disease may influence outcome.

ISCHAEMIC HEART DISEASE

The major risk factors for ischaemic or coronary heart disease include high blood pressure, high plasma cholesterol concentration and cigarette smoking. However, the presence of these risk factors alone does not account for all cases, and a psychosocial component has long been suspected. One group that has received particular attention are Japanese living in different countries. For an indus-trialised country, Japan has a very low rate of ischaemic heart disease, but rates are higher among Japanese people living in Hawaii, and even higher among those who live in California. Although dietary factors are implicated, social networks may also be relevant. Traditional Japanese culture has high levels of social support, with close families and loyalty to occupational and cultural groups. The role of this factor in ischaemic heart disease has been tested by classifying Japanese men living in California according to a number of measures of cultural integration. It was found that the prevalence of ischaemic heart disease was lowest among men who retained a strong Japanese identity and remained within this ethnic group. Disease rates were higher in those who were assimi-lated into Western culture, and the differences were not explained by changes in smoking, diet or other risk factors. A number of other studies have shown that rates of ischaemic heart disease are higher in those who move out of stable, cohesive cultures into new strata of society where their status is uncertain. However, in addition to social and cultural influences, personal characteristics play an important role.

Type A coronary-prone behaviour

Type A behaviour is a habitual behavioural style that has been shown by the American cardiologists Friedman & Rosenman to increase the risk of ischaemic heart disease. Type A characteristics include sustained aggression or hostility, ambition, competitiveness and a chronic sense of time urgency. People showing the type A pattern are also described as impatient, constantly alert and intensely committed to their jobs or occupations. People who do not show these characteristics are described as Type B. The importance of this factor was demonstrated in a large prospective study, in which more than 3000 disease-free men in California were followed up for $8\frac{1}{2}$ years. Over this period, ischaemic heart disease (fatal and non-fatal myocardial infarction or angina pectoris) developed at twice the rate in type A compared with type B men. The standard risk factors were also reliable predictors in this survey, but did not account for the link between type A behaviour and morbidity. Other studies have since shown that type A behaviour is relevant in women.

Type A is generally considered to be a behaviour pattern rather than a fixed personality trait. The reason for this is that type A characteristics are not present all the time, but only emerge when people are confronted by challenging situations. In the presence of challenges, particularly when they are competitive in nature, type A individuals work more intensely. Type A ratings are high among hospital doctors and business school graduates, compared with people in less hard-driving occupations, suggesting that competitive environments may foster the behaviour pattern. Moreover, several studies have shown that when type A individuals are confronted by demanding situations, they show larger blood pressure and catecholamine reactions than type B people. Figure 7.5 outlines the psychophysiological processes that may explain the link between type A behaviour and ischaemic heart disease.

Changing type A behaviour

If type A behaviour is an important risk factor, perhaps changing people in the type B direction would reduce rates of ischaemic

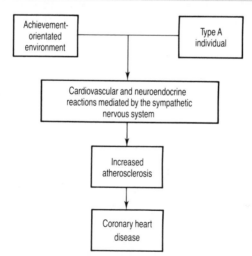

Fig. 7.5 Hypothetical scheme linking coronary-prone behaviour with heart disease.

heart disease. Efforts have been concentrated on changing type A behaviour among people who have already had a heart attack. Such individuals are strongly motivated to change, and the danger to them of staying at high risk is considerable. A large study has recently been carried out in which several hundred postinfarction patients were randomly assigned to type A intervention and medical counselling groups. The type A intervention groups met regularly, and a variety of behavioural and cognitive psychological treatment methods were used to modify the behaviour pattern. The medical counselling groups also met for several sessions, but were advised about standard cardiac risks and not type A behaviour. Over a 3-year follow-up period, there were significantly fewer new heart attacks in the type A intervention condition. Measures of type A behaviour were also lower in the latter group, suggesting that modifying type A behaviour is feasible, and may lead to reduced coronary risk.

THE STRESS–DIATHESIS MODEL

Several different influences of psychosocial factors on medical disorders have been outlined. However, not everyone exposed to extreme life stress succumbs to illness. Furthermore, the illness response is variable; some people may develop high blood pressure, for instance, while others may become seriously depressed. This suggests that psychosocial factors interact with organic or physiological predispositions in the development of illness. A general interactional stress–diathesis (predisposition) model is summarised

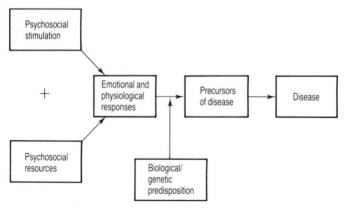

Fig. 7.6 Stress-diathesis model of illness.

in Figure 7.6. This shows that psychosocial stimulation does not inevitably produce emotional and physiological responses, since it is modulated by the resources of the individual (coping responses, social supports, etc). Psychophysiological responses will only stimulate disease processes in the biologically vulnerable. Such vulnerability may be genetic in origin, or may be acquired during life. Thus one person may have a hypertensive family history and be prone to cardiovascular disease, while another may have airways hyper-reactivity, so tend to respond with bronchoconstriction. The importance of these processes varies across individuals, so it is not helpful to talk about a specific group of psychosomatic disorders. Rather, psychosocial factors may be involved in *all* medical disorders to a greater or lesser extent.

It should also be recalled that behaviour exerts an immense influence on health outside the pathways discussed here. Habitual behaviours such as cigarette smoking, physical exercise, alcohol and drug abuse and risk taking are major causes of death and disease in our society. The modification of these behaviours is detailed in Chapter 11.

BIOFEEDBACK AND RELAXATION TRAINING

Autonomic responses are generally considered to be involuntary, occurring automatically in the maintenance of physiological homeostasis. However, self-control techniques can be used to modify autonomic and other physiological responses. In biofeedback, a physiological parameter (e.g. heart rate or muscle tension) is monitored, converted to an easily understood display, and a feedback loop is set up, as shown in Figure 7.7. With this augmented feedback loop, subjects are able to detect changes in activity of which they are not normally aware. The method has been used for training in self-control of cardiovascular variables (heart rate, blood-pressure or blood-flow), EEG parameters such as alpha wave frequency, muscle tension in various areas of the body, and other functions such as pulmonary resistance and gastric acid secretion.

It is not clear how control is produced with biofeedback. One idea is that it is a form of operant conditioning (Chapter 3), where a physiological response is reinforced by the feedback. In addition, it shares some properties with the learning of skilled motor tasks such as throwing darts. When we learn skilled activities of this type, the frequency and quality of performance feedback is critical; if you only knew about the outcome of every other throw, you

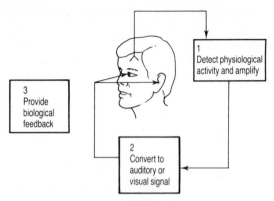

Fig. 7.7 A schematic model of the biofeedback process, in which bioelectrical potentials are detected and converted to sensory information.

would not learn to play darts very fast. Biofeedback may also work by enhancing the person's awareness of physiological activity. It may permit people to test different ways of producing somatic changes, enabling the consequences of each strategy to be assessed.

Clinical applications

Clinically, biofeedback has been used in two ways:
(a) As a method of gaining *specific control* over certain functions that are not normally regulated voluntarily. Bronchial asthmatics may be trained to control their airways resistance, epileptics their EEG activity, and people with neuromuscular disorders their muscle tonus. Migraine and cardiac arrhythmias have been treated in the same way. In each case, the aim is to develop voluntary control so that patients can contribute to their own treatment instead of relying on drugs. Not all of these applications have been tested rigorously, and this treatment may have very strong placebo components.
(b) As an index of more *general relaxation*. Thus biofeedback of muscle tension and sweat gland activity may be provided to help people relax more deeply.

When biofeedback is used in this second way, it is generally accompanied by instructional methods of self-control such as relaxation and meditation. *Relaxation training* usually takes place over several sessions with a therapist or taped instructions. The commonest methods are progressive muscle relaxation, in which patients learn to tense and relax different muscle groups in turn, and autogenic training. The latter is similar to self-hypnosis, in that subjects repeat a series of statements to themselves suggesting physical warmth and heaviness. There are many different types of meditation training, but their physiological effects are relatively uniform, with reduced oxygen consumption, muscle tone and sweat gland activity accompanied by shifts in the EEG spectrum towards lower frequencies.

When these methods are used clinically, efforts are made to transfer the effects of training into everyday life. Thus subjects are encouraged to relax whenever they feel tension building up during ordinary activities. These methods are used not only in the management of emotional disorders (see Chapter 9) and insomnia (see Chapter 2), but also in the treatment of headache, essential hypertension and tension problems. Table 7.1 summarises the blood pressure responses of hypertensive patients assigned at random to relaxation plus biofeedback training and control conditions. Following twelve 30-minute sessions, blood pressure in the control group had fallen to a slight but significant degree, confirming the influence of placebo effects. However, the reduction in the treatment group was very much greater, with normalisation of blood pressure in many patients. Similar effects have been found to persist even at 4 years after the training period.

For many conditions, biofeedback does not appear to add to the effect produced by relaxation training alone. Since biofeedback requires some electronic equipment, it is often more economical to use relaxation methods. These techniques may be increasingly used in the future as more patients are identified with chronic problems such as essential hypertension, in which they may otherwise face decades of treatment with drugs. The application of psychological methods in the management of organic disease has come to be known as *behavioural medicine*.

Table 7.1 Changes in blood-pressure with biofeedback-assisted relaxation training

	Mean initial BP	Mean final BP	Drop in systolic BP	Drop in diastolic BP
Treatment (n = 17)	167.5/99.6	141.4/84.4	26.1	15.2
Control (n = 17)	168.9/100.6	160.0/96.4	8.9	4.2

From Patel & North (1975)

FURTHER READING

Gentry W D (ed) 1984 Handbook of behavioral medicine. Guilford Press, New York
Henry J P, Stephens P M 1977 Stress, health, and the social environment. Springer, New York
Steptoe A, Mathews A (eds) 1984 Health care and human behaviour. Academic Press, London

STUDY QUESTIONS

1. Why is it difficult to draw firm conclusions about stress-related illness from a retrospective study?
2. What links exist between ischaemic heart disease and behaviour?
3. What physical changes occur during a stress reaction?
4. How is biofeedback related to relaxation?
5. What are the applications of stress-reduction techniques in medical disorders?
6. Describe the influence of life events on health and disease.

8

The psychology of pain

In his book *Pain mechanisms*, published in 1943, William Living-stone wrote that he was:

> brought up in a medical generation in which. . . pain was (considered to be) a primary sensation dependent upon the stimu-lation of a specific sensory ending by a stimulus of a certain inten-sity, and conducted along a fixed pathway to ring a special bell in consciousness. Pain was as simple as that . . . The idea that anything might happen to sensory impulses within the central nervous system to alter their character, destination, or the sensation they registered in consciousness was utterly foreign to my concept. But in practice I found that it was incredibly difficult to make this concept consistent with clinical observations.

Pain is primarily a signal that body tissues have been damaged, and serves to promote the avoidance of further damage. The experience combines sensory qualities, indicating the exact location of damage, an unpleasant emotional state, and related 'pain behav-iour' such as avoidance. While this aversive quality is usually biologically adaptive, it may sometimes cease to serve any useful purpose, and becomes a medical problem in its own right (e.g. terminal cancer pain). On the other hand, the rare conditions of congenital insensitivity to pain, in which severe and extensive injuries are tolerated without distress (despite adequate sensory location) reveals its biological protective function. Such unfortunate individuals usually sustain severe injuries through self-neglect, and do not survive long.

Effects of context

The experience of pain also seems to depend on the environmental and emotional circumstances in which it occurs. In the hook-hanging ritual performed in India, for example, a villager who has been chosen to bless the children and the crops in neighbouring villages allows a large hook to be thrust under the muscles of his back. At the climax of the ceremony he hangs from a rope attached to the hook while showing exultation rather than pain. A similar absence of pain has been described in other religious rituals, during intense action in emergencies, and in hypnotic or other trance states. It thus appears that the perception of pain can be greatly modified by emotional state, by the significance of the situation, or by competing demands for attention. Further evidence showing that the extent of injury has no simple relationship with the amount of pain experienced comes from medical conditions where pain is the main symptom.

PATHOLOGICAL PAIN SYNDROMES

Phantom limb pain

Following amputation it is common for the patient to report sensations from a missing part as if it were still present. In 5 to 10% of these cases the phantom limb is experienced as painful. The limb may commonly feel as though fixed in an uncomfortable position, and pain is associated with this position or the injury that led to the amputation (according to one patient 'as if a sharp object were being driven repeatedly into the site of the original wound'). Section of relevant afferent nerves can sometimes bring relief, but in a few striking cases even complete section of the spinal cord to prevent fibres from the damaged areas reaching the brain may leave the pain unaltered. Alternative treatments that may be successful include temporary anaesthetic block to the stump or progressively more vigorous sensory stimulation to the same area.

Causalgia and neuralgias

Sensory fibres are traditionally divided into three types: A-beta or large myelinated, A-delta or small myelinated, and C or small unmyelinated fibres. After nerve damage caused by acute trauma such as a bullet wound, chronic burning pain (causalgia) can persist for years after healing is apparently complete. Innocuous stimulation at points remote from the site of injury may trigger intense pain, which is often worsened by emotional circumstances. The multiple regeneration of small diameter nerve fibres that were torn in the original trauma may be implicated in such cases.

Diseases causing selective damage to large diameter myelinated fibres may also lead to persistent pain (neuralgia).

Repeated application of light-touch stimuli to trigger points causes little sensation at first, but then can lead to a slowly rising and extremely severe pain.

NEUROPSYCHOLOGICAL MECHANISMS OF PAIN

Such clinical observations led Melzack (a Canadian psychologist) & Wall (a British physiologist) to reject previous simple views of pain which assumed that the stimulation of specific receptors or free-ending *nocieptors* by tissue damage led directly to pain. They argued that, since pain could be increased either by the abnormal regeneration of small diameter fibres or by selective loss of large fibres, the balance between input from both types must determine the extent to which pain signals are transmitted to the brain. The existence of phantom limb pain, and especially the occasional failure to arrest it despite complete spinal section, suggested that pain may be represented by neuronal networks at higher levels in the central nervous system and that discharge from such networks could re-activate previous pain experiences ('pain memories'). Finally, they argued that the inhibition of pain by certain psychological states indicated that pain signals could be inhibited by descending controls from the brain. The mechanism proposed by Melzack & Wall in 1965 to account for these effects was a 'gate' in the spinal cord, which was normally open to allow pain impulses to get through, but when activated could close to prevent onward transmission.

Gate theory

The proposed gate control system in the substantia gelatinosia (SG) of the dorsal horns is said to accept input from large or small fibres, both of which serve to excite pain transmission (T) cells that project to the brain (see Fig. 8.1). However, while large fibres (A-beta) also stimulate inhibitory gate cells in the SG, small fibres (A-delta or C) have the opposite effect. Since gate cell activity tends to prevent pain impulses from being transmitted to the brain, small fibre activity promotes onward pain transmission, while large fibres damp down transmission by closing the gate. Tissue damage excites both large and small fibres: the large myelinated sensory fibres acting rapidly but with only transient effect, the thin myelinated A-delta fibres leading to 'pin-prick' pain and reflex withdrawal, and the small unmyelinated C fibres causing slower but more persistent

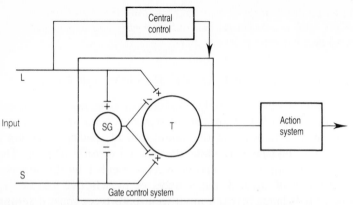

Fig. 8.1 The first version of the gate control theory (From 'The Challenge of Pain' by Melzack and Wall (1982), Penguin, Harmondsworth, p 226. Reproduced by permission of Penguin Books Ltd.)

pain signals. Re-instating large fibre activity, for example by scratching near to the site of injury, will thus tend to damp pain down for a short while.

The theory assigns an important role to descending controls from higher centres that in some way serve to regulate the state of the gate system. Cortical activity arising from a positive interpretation of the painful stimulation, or a situation demanding urgent action, will activate these descending controls and close the gate.

Evaluation of gate theory

Gate theory has not been accepted without criticism. Cases of hereditary insensitivity to pain have been found that are associated with the loss of large and medium myelinated fibres, but with preserved C fibres. Similarly, diseases that destroy large fibres do not always produce chronic pain, contrary to the predictions to gate theory. The original theory stated that substantia gelatinosia cells inhibit transmission cells via presynaptic control, but it is now believed that postsynaptic control also occurs. Despite such problems, it is generally accepted that pain is determined by the interaction of different types of sensory input at spinal level, and that descending pathways from the brain can facilitate or inhibit its onward transmission (see Fig. 8.2). Gate theory has also led to important advances in the treatment of chronic pain. Persistent pain following injury, for example, can sometimes be successfully treated by using transcutaneous nerve stimulators — portable

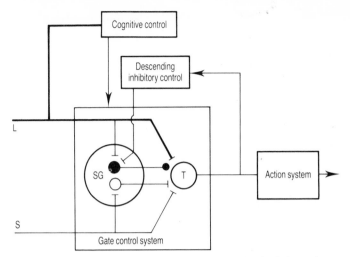

Fig. 8.2 The second version of the gate control theory. This includes excitatory (○) and inhibitory (●) links from SG, and leaves open the pre- or postsynaptic action of the inhibitory link to the T cells. Separate cognitive and brain stem inhibitory controls are shown, although these may well be connected. (From 'The Challenge of Pain' by Melzack and Wall (1982), Penguin, Harmondsworth, p 235. Reproduced by permission of Penguin Books Ltd.)

devices that produce electrical impulses which selectively stimulate large sensory fibres.

Brain systems involved in pain perception

The fact that pain has both sensory-localising properties, and an unpleasant emotional quality, suggests that more than one brain system is involved. Following operations that cut thalamic connections to the forebrain (frontal lobotomy), patients can still feel noxious stimuli (and in fact sensory thresholds may be slightly lower) but sometimes report that the previously severe pain does not bother them so much. There would thus appear to be two major pathways at brain level, one dealing with sensory discrimination and the other with emotional response. True pain is felt only when both are active simultaneously.

On the emotional side (left hand of Figure 8.3) pathways ascend the dorsal column and project to the reticular formation of the brain stem, the limbic midbrain area and the medial thalamus, from where they continue on to the limbic forebrain structures and frontal cortex. On the sensory discrimination side (right hand of Fig. 8.3) the relèvant pathways project via the thalamus to the

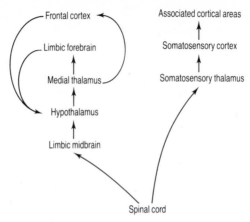

Fig. 8.3 Ascending pathways from the gate control system to the brain, showing emotional (left-hand) and sensory (right-hand) mediating routes.

sensory cortex and associated cortical areas, from where (and from the brain stem) descending pathways to the spinal cord also originate.

Descending controls and endogenous opiates

Although the existence of central control over the gate was postulated by Melzack & Wall (1965) on the basis of psychological evidence, the recent discovery of opiate-like substances (endorphins) in the central nervous system has provided additional evidence and a possible mechanism. Micro-injection of endorphins into the central grey of the brain stem causes a marked degree of analgesia, and a similar reduction of pain is observed in animals following electrical stimulation to the same area. Certain types of severe environmental stress also appear to result in endorphin-induced analgesia. These endogenous pain-inhibitory systems are subject to learning, since a conditioned analgesia can be induced to a stimulus that normally signals shock delivery.

In humans, *placebo analgesia* (reduction of pain following dummy medication) has been attributed to similar mechanisms, since the placebo effect has been reported to be reduced by administration of naloxone, an opiate antagonist. While the latter effect has proved difficult to replicate, the combined evidence strongly suggests that central nervous system activity associated with either positive expectations, emotion or stress can trigger endorphin release in the brain stem and cause partial analgesia for pain. In terms of gate theory, this implies that endogenous opiates are involved in the central controls that serve to close the spinal gate. However, the descending pathway from the brain stem to gate control system in the dorsal horn is itself serotoninergic (i.e. has 5-HT as a neurotransmitter). Interestingly, opiates appear to inhibit only slowly rising persistent pain, but not transient 'pin-prick' pain, suggesting that only the former is subject to descending controls involving endorphins.

PAIN AND OTHER PSYCHOLOGICAL PROCESSES

Pain is a subjective and personal experience that is influenced by many other associated psychological processes. The intensity with which pain is experienced can only be measured by subjective report, although this can be done using standardised rating scales to allow the assessment of changes over time or with treatment. Pain is also expressed by characteristic behaviours, such as wincing and avoidance, which are also subject to psychological influences such as learning (see below).

The effect of learning

Animals reared in isolation and protected from noxious stimuli of any kind do not react normally to their first encounter with painful stimuli. Such animals may not flinch from pin pricks, and will sniff repeatedly at a candle flame before learning to leave it alone.

Pavlovian conditioning with escalating pain stimulation as the CS and food as the UCS (see Chapter 3) may lead to apparently 'masochistic' animals that react to quite painful stimuli with apparent pleasure. Thus, although pain mechanisms are innate, when and how pain is expressed can be modified by learning.

In humans, the *pain threshold* (the point at which pain is first reported) seems fairly constant, but *pain tolerance* (the point at which pain is avoided) seems to be more influenced by learning. Men are expected to show high tolerance and are reinforced for it in comparison to women. Hence, although both men and women patients rated postsurgical pain similarly in one study, nurses gave male patients significantly fewer analgesics.

Social learning of pain behaviour

Some cultural groups accept or even encourage free expression of pain more than others, and these groups tend to be characterised by lower pain tolerance. Thus, one study found that Italians and Jewish Americans tolerate pain less well than 'old' Americans, perhaps as a result of early social learning.

Some evidence for social learning effects arises from experiments in which subjects have their pain tolerance assessed when alone or with another subject who displays a great deal of pain behaviour or with a subject who minimises their pain. Tolerance was decreased in the presence of a demonstrative subject, and increased by the presence of a stoical companion.

Pain behaviour on medical wards

In the clinical context, this research would imply that observation of others on a ward who are experiencing severe pain might lead patients to tolerate their own pain less well. Pain behaviour in chronic patients may also sometimes come under operant control, so that grimaces, moaning and the like may be inadvertently reinforced by nursing staff. In one such patient who was noted to display pain behaviour only in the presence of staff, experimental periods of social reinforcement (conversing and showing approval) for other activities, interspersed with a return to baseline, showed how this can be treated (see Fig. 8.4).

Pain and emotional state

Pain is subjectively increased in anxious and depressed patients, perhaps because the emotional aspects of pain are closely integrated

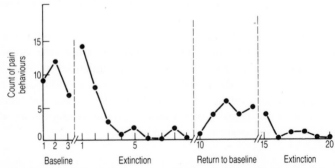

Fig. 8.4 Record of pain behaviour for a 47-year-old chronic back-pain patient, showing the effect of staff attention to pain behaviour (reinforcement) and attention to incompatible behaviour (non-reinforcement) (from Fordyce 1976).

with emotional disturbance caused in other ways. Chronic pain can sometimes be alleviated by antidepressant medication, and reduction of pre-operative anxiety leads to decreases in postoperative pain (see Chapter 6). Psychological measures of the predisposition to experience negative emotions (neuroticism or trait anxiety, see Chapter 5) can be used to predict which patients will experience above average postoperative pain and will take longer to recover. Emotion and pain would thus appear to be inextricably entangled.

Attention, expectation and pain perception

The extent to which sensory information is perceived depends heavily on selective attention to it, and pain is no exception. When the person is preoccupied by other important tasks the perception of pain is diminished, while focusing attention on painful stimuli increases their apparent effects. Most experimental studies thus find that distraction reduces distress, although selective attention to the noxious stimulation does not always increase pain provided the subject interprets the sensations in a positive way. The way in which the perception of pain often depends on an interaction between attention and expectations is illustrated in the following experiment.

To investigate the claims that white noise (all frequency sound) was useful in dental analgesia, some patients listened to intense white noise combined with suggestions that it would relieve pain, some were exposed to white noise without positive suggestions, and some were given suggestions of pain relief alone. Neither of the last two conditions were effective in comparison to the first. Questioning subjects in the combined condition revealed that they deliberately concentrated on the noise in the belief that this would help in controlling pain. Since noise alone did not reduce pain, this experiment shows that positive expectations may be useful to the extent that they direct attention to other sources of sensory stimulation.

Pain and placebo

Placebos (dummy medication) have often been shown to have powerful medical and psychological effects, including the reduction of pain. In controlled trials, placebos tend to reduce pain by about one-third to one-half as much as any specific analgesic with which they are being compared. The reason for the widespread effectiveness of placebos remains unclear, but the following possibilities exist:

(a) After repeated administration of an active drug to animals, a similar dummy administration sometimes produces conditioned responses that resemble those of the actual drug. However, other experiments have shown that some drugs (such as morphine) lead to conditioning of an antagonistic homeostatic response, which is opposite in direction to the usual drug reaction (see Chapter 3). Thus conditioned 'placebo' effects may sometimes resemble and sometimes oppose the original drug effect.

(b) Placebos almost certainly have emotional effects, such as increasing hope and decreasing anxiety and depression. While these mood changes may not abolish pain, they are known to reduce it and make it more tolerable.

(c) Since the magnitude of placebo responses varies with the expectations of the patients (as conveyed by the doctor), it may well be that positive expectancy has direct effects on the brain system involved in pain perception. However, the evidence reviewed above makes it more likely that expectations operate via changes in selective attention, and reduction in other behaviours that serve to maintain pain.

Any full explanation of placebo action must take into account mechanisms other than those involved in pain, since placebos can have effects on many other psychological and physiological functions.

THE PSYCHOLOGICAL MANAGEMENT OF PERSISTENT PAIN

Headache

Methods such as muscle relaxation, often augmented with auditory biofeedback of the electromyogram (EMG) recorded from muscles such as the frontalis (see Chapter 7), have been widely used with so-called tension headaches. Although biofeedback has been found to be effective in controlled trials, the improvement in headache is not always closely correlated with the extent of EMG reduction, which casts doubt on the precise role of excessive muscle tension in the aetiology of headache.

Migraine headaches, which are thought to result from cranial vascular constriction followed by dilation, have also been treated using biofeedback of vascular changes. While also often effective, current evidence suggests that such treatments work by teaching patients to become more relaxed generally, and to avoid behaviours that lead to headaches, rather than via specific physiological changes alone.

Chronic pain

Acute pain that continues only while tissue damage is present can be distinguished from chronic pain syndromes in which complaints of pain persist well past the time that healing is apparently complete. As chronicity continues, so pain behaviours such as analgesic abuse and inactivity tend to become more prominent. One reason for this is that such responses serve to reduce distress temporarily as well as attract sympathy, and are thus reinforced. However, in the long term these pain behaviours are maladaptive since they may lead to analgesic tolerance and addiction, a focus on pain sensations and a reduction in alternative sources of sensory input, all of which may actually serve to maintain chronic pain. For this reason, the management of persistent pain sometimes requires psychological as well as medical treatment.

Operant treatment programmes

Patients showing persistent pain behaviour in the absence of organic pathology sufficient to account for the problem may be treated using operant learning principles developed in the United States by Fordyce, a behavioural psychologist. Dependence on dangerously high levels of analgesic medication is first reduced by mixing all drugs being taken into an anonymous 'pain cocktail' which is given at fixed intervals rather than on demand. This avoids the reinforcement of complaint behaviours. The active ingredients may than be gradually reduced, usually without provoking excessive protest or withdrawal symptoms.

At the same time, family members and hospital staff are instructed to ignore (extinguish) other maladaptive pain behaviour, such as lying down and avoiding all exercise. Instead, social reinforcement such as praise and attention is directed towards activities incompatible with exclusive attention being paid to the pain. Graded exercise programmes are constructed for each individual so that patients can monitor their own progress and be encouraged by others to achieve successively higher activity targets. Although such programmes usually increase tolerance and reduce level of pain rather than abolishing it completely, in many cases they have proved the only means whereby a bedridden chronic pain patient was able to resume a normal, active life.

Terminal pain

Pain relief is the single most important feature in terminal cancer care, but until recently it was unfortunately neglected. It is now widely recognised that this is best achieved in a specialised institution (the hospice), of the sort pioneered by Dr Cicily Saunders in London. In a hospice the emphasis is on relief of suffering rather than cure, allowing fears about death to be dealt with in the absence of pain. The most useful medication for terminal pain relief is morphine, which is given in various forms, together with other drugs such as phenothiazines to control nausea and anxiety. Dependence and tolerance on opiates is not a problem under such circumstances. Rather than being given on demand, which implies that pain has already broken through drug control, medication must be given on a regular schedule so that the next dose is given just before the last has worn off (about every 3–4 hours). The hospice movement, and the systematic use of opiates in terminal pain control, has shown that dying does not need to be unpleasant and can usually be faced calmly and with dignity.

FURTHER READING

Holzman A, Turk D 1986 Pain management. Pergamon Press, New York
McCaul K, Malott J 1984 Distraction and coping with pain. Psychological Bulletin 95: 516–533
Melzack R, Wall P 1982 The challenge of pain. Penguin, Harmondsworth

STUDY QUESTIONS

1. Distinguish between:
   (a) pain experience and pain behaviour;
   (b) pain threshold and pain tolerance;
   (c) fast and slow pain;
   (d) acute and chronic pain.
2. List the clinical pain problems that have been mentioned in this chapter. What has been learned from them about the nature of pain?
3. What evidence has been found for or against gate theory as formulated by Melzack & Wall in 1965?
4. What brain mechanisms (above the spinal cord) are involved in the reaction to painful stimuli?

5. How do you think placebos work? (Remember that placebos can do more than reduce pain.)

6. An American surgeon, working during the Second World War, observed that severely wounded soldiers leaving the front line complained little of pain and often refused morphine. In contrast, the same men receiving surgery after the war complained vociferously about pain. What explanations can you think of to account for this difference?

9

Emotional disorders and psychological treatments

Severe forms of mental illness, such as schizophrenia, are relatively rare (affecting only about 1% of the population) but usually require hospitalisation and specialised psychiatric treatment. These *psychotic* conditions involve unusual symptoms such as hallucinations and delusions, indicating a loss of contact with reality. By contrast, this chapter will concern *neurotic* disturbances of mood (anxiety and depression), psychosomatic conditions (such as headaches, insomnia and sexual problems) and disturbances of personality or behaviour (such as antisocial aggression and alcohol and drug abuse). These emotional and behavioural disorders are extremely common, being present in varying degrees and at different times in a large proportion of the population. Whereas psychoses such as schizophrenia may best be understood as neurological or neurochemical disorders, these common emotional and behavioural problems are more likely to arise from maladaptive emotional learning, and thus may be thought of and treated as psychological problems. However, the majority of such patients will never see a psychiatrist, but instead may present in general practice or in hospital clinics.

Psychological problems in medical practice

Physical conditions and their medical treatment are a common source of psychological problems, although doctors often remain unaware of their existence. For example, many patients will become extremely anxious at the prospect of surgery or such invasive investigations as cardiac catheterisation. Many other treatments involve regular exposure to aversive situations, as with cancer patients who must undergo chemotherapy that induces nausea. Many such patients acquire such powerful conditioned 'phobias' that they may vomit as the time for each dose approaches. Understandably, terminal illness is also often associated with severe depression in both patient and relatives.

Other less serious but chronic conditions require changes in diet, activity level or life-style that create problems of behavioural and emotional adjustment. The application of learning and other psychological principles to the management of physical illness has become known as *behavioural medicine* (see Chapters 7 and 11).

EPIDEMIOLOGY OF EMOTIONAL DISORDERS

Anxiety and depression are normal emotional experiences under the appropriate circumstances. However, as emotional distress begins to be out of proportion to the objective circumstances, and associated with behavioural disturbance sufficient to interfere with normal life, we tend to refer to anxiety or depression as *disorders*. The prevalence of emotional disorder therefore depends on the choice of an arbitrary cut-off point along a continuous distribution of distress and disturbance. For example, in one survey in which new town residents were questioned about excessive nervousness, depression, sleeplessness or irritability, 33% reported at least one such symptom, 8% were receiving some form of treatment for these symptoms, 4% were being seen as psychiatric out-patients and 2% had received psychiatric in-patient care at some time in their lives. Emotional disorders may thus be said to affect between 33% and 2% of the population, depending on the criterion used.

In a survey of general patients in London, 9% of all those consulting their GP were considered to be suffering from a neurotic disorder, with rather more women in the sample (12%) than men (6%). Such figures may be regarded as conservative, since the proportion of the population who have been prescribed psychotropic drugs (e.g. antidepressants, tranquillisers, sedatives) in 1 year was found to be considerably higher (18%).

Cultural differences

Surprisingly similar levels of diagnosed neurotic disturbances have been reported across different cultures, such as African villages where it was reported as 9%, although the way in which the symptoms manifested may be strikingly different. In the condition known as 'Koro' by Malay–Chinese, for example, epidemics of acute anxiety are associated with the belief that the genitals of afflicted men may contract into the abdomen, with fatal consequences. Epidemic forms of acute anxiety are not unknown in

Western countries, and outbreaks of nausea and fainting have sometimes threatened to close down schools, despite the lack of any physical cause. Susceptible individuals tend to be young females, and to have high extraversion and neuroticism scores (see Chapter 5).

TYPES OF EMOTIONAL DISORDER

Anxiety disorders

Common conditions considered under the general heading of anxiety include specific fears or *phobias*, generalised anxiety disorders and related conditions characterised by acute attacks of panic in the absence of sufficient external cause. The reactions accompanying such abnormal anxiety states resemble those that occur in normal fear, namely subjective alarm and increased physiological activation, as if in preparation for 'flight or fight'. However, while individuals with specific phobias show such reactions only in the presence of feared stimuli (such as spiders, heights, social situations, etc.), those suffering from generalised anxiety states typically show elevated arousal much of the time. At the same time generalised anxiety disorders are accompanied by frequent thoughts about personal danger, such as possible social failure, disease or even death. Normal individuals react to a sudden noise by showing a marked autonomic reaction, but repeated applications of the same noise causes a rapid loss of response (*habituation*) (see Fig. 9.1). On the other hand, patients with anxiety states fail to show habituation, and respond persistently as long as the noise is repeated. This pattern occurs only in generalised anxiety and not in people having specific phobias, whose reactions resemble those of non-anxious people.

Phobic states

A phobic state is usually said to exist if a person fears and avoids situations to an extent sufficient to disturb their normal life, despite knowing that such situations are objectively harmless. Agoraphobia appears to lie between phobias of specific stimuli and generalised anxiety states. Agoraphobics experience fear of being far from home, particularly when alone, or of entering crowded public places. They also seem to be vulnerable to acute attacks of panic, and their physiological reactions sometimes approach those of anxiety states.

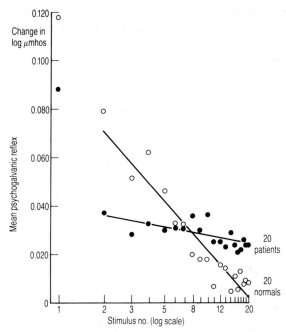

Fig. 9.1 Skin conductance responses to 20 repeated tones in anxiety state patients and controls, showing more rapid habituation in controls than in patients (From Lader and Wing (1966), 'Psychological Measures, Sedative Drugs and Marked Anxiety', Oxford University Press. Reprinted with permission.)

Women are about three times more likely than men to complain of specific fears or agoraphobia, although social fears and generalised anxiety states are almost equally divided between the sexes. Onset age also differs across conditions, with specific fears usually beginning very early (mean onset age of 4 years). Social fears follow adolescence (mean onset 19 years), with other anxiety states and agoraphobia tending to begin in early adulthood (mean onset 25 years). Specific fears thus begin earlier and tend to affect women more, but are not accompanied by any obvious autonomic disturbance, in contrast to more generalised forms of anxiety.

Role of anxiety in other conditions

This can be illustrated by considering an apparently distinct behavioural problem: obsessive–compulsive neurosis. This is a rare condition in which an individual feels compelled to repeat a thought or act, despite knowing that it is inappropriate. The most common compulsions relate to cleanliness, and may take the form of rituals such as washing the hands repeatedly following supposed contamination. After touching something that they feel is dirty (such as a door handle), the obsessional person experiences a feeling of discomfort until the contamination is removed. Anxiety aroused by thoughts of contamination thus seem to be important in the development of compulsive behaviour, although its origins are not yet fully understood. In a similar way, other problems such as alcohol abuse may sometimes begin as a maladaptive attempt to deal with social anxiety, or psychosomatic symptoms may result from particular types of somatic anxiety response.

Depressive disorders

In depressive disorders the normal emotion of sadness is deepened by a sense of hopelessness and worthlessness, often leading to total inactivity. Common accompanying symptoms include loss of energy, reduced appetite for food or interest in sex, and disturbed sleep. Suicidal thoughts are common, and the majority of successful suicides were severely depressed at the time of taking their lives.

The symptoms of depression seem to fall into two general clusters, with appetite loss, early morning wakening and motor retardation being characteristic of one type, and lack of these features together with previous neurotic personality traits being more typical of the other. The former type (sometimes misleadingly called endogenous as opposed to reactive depression) is more likely to occur late in life, and may respond better to physical treatment such as electroconvulsive therapy. However, there is no evidence that the two types differ in their causes.

AETIOLOGICAL FACTORS IN EMOTIONAL DISORDERS

Genetic factors

Although genetic factors do not determine the exact form of disorder, they influence the probability that any emotional problem will occur, given appropriate circumstances. If emotionally reactive (or non-reactive) animals are selected and systematically inbred, two distinctly different strains emerge. Those in the reactive strain are considerably more autonomically responsive to aversive stimuli than are the non-reactive individuals, despite exposure to an identical environment.

In humans, questionnaire measures of neuroticism (see Chapter 5) show that monozygotic twins are more similar ($r = 0.5$) than are dizygotic twins ($r = 0.3$). Also, if one twin has suffered an emotional disorder already, then the risk of the other also suffering one is significantly increased. In one such study, the risk for the second twin to experience some disorder (although not necessarily the same one) was raised to 47% in monozygotic pairs and 24% in dizygotic pairs. The difference between these two probabilities strongly suggests the contribution of genetic factors, although their extent varies across conditions and more than half of the variation remains to be accounted for by other factors, presumably environmental.

Environmental factors

Direct experiments on the aetiology of emotional disorders can only be conducted in animals, and obviously these may not relate directly to human neuroses. So-called experimental neuroses in animals (see Chapter 3) can be readily induced by the use of unpredictable electric shock, physical confinement, severe over-crowding or conflict between incompatible responses. Isolation of an infant monkey from its mother and peers is followed by an initial stage of protest, and later by apparent despair in which the infant becomes unresponsive to stimulation and adopts a huddled self-clasping posture resembling depression. If prolonged, such severe treatment leaves the monkey unable to regain normal social or sexual responsiveness in later life. Instead of showing interest when re-introduced to other monkeys, it may appear frightened and withdrawn. Those monkeys that do become parents after such treatment seem unable to respond appropriately even to their own offspring.

Despite difficulties in generalising to humans, follow-up studies of children who have been separated from their mothers (for example by hospitalisation) show that prolonged isolation between the ages of 2 and 5 years may be associated with a greater incidence of later behavioural disturbance, although lesser degrees of sep-aration have little or no effect. Severe trauma in adults is also followed by a marked increase in depression or anxiety often persisting for years. For example, people involved in natural disasters or who are the victims of criminal assault frequently show a greatly raised incidence of later anxiety states, while the death of a close family member is associated with increased vulnerability to depression. Clearly, neither genetic nor environmental influence can provide complete explanations of emotional disorders. Rather it is an interaction between the two, such that genetically vulnerable individuals will tend to develop emotional disorders should they be subjected to appropriately stressful situations.

THEORIES OF EMOTIONAL DISORDER

Although there is general agreement that genetic and environmental influences interact in causing emotional disorders, there is no such agreement as to the precise nature of the mechanisms involved. These are undoubtedly multifactorial, but this has not prevented the development of unrelated theories. Each of these competing theories will therefore be examined first, before attempting an integration between them.

Psychodynamic theories

While mainly of historical interest, Freud and other psychoanalytic theorists were none the less important in suggesting that neuroses may arise from early learning of which we may remain unaware. Painful experiences, such as conflicts concerning unacceptable guilt over sexual feelings, were supposed to be shut out from awareness by a process termed *repression*. The form of neurotic symptoms that might arise later was said to depend on the nature of the repressed, but still active, subconscious memories. Hence anxiety might arise should something threaten to remind a person of a conflict involving punishment. Depression was thought to be a consequence of repressed aggression, which may then be turned inward against oneself, or in later theories as the consequence of repressed memories of the painful loss of a loved object or person. Unfortunately, psychoanalytic ideas have generally been cast in too vague a form to make them scientifically testable.

Neuropharmacological approaches

At the opposite theoretical pole, recent evidence implicates changes in neurotransmission function, such as levels of biogenic amines (see Table 9.1). Drugs that deplete brain amines such as noradrenaline can cause depression, while drugs that prevent their reuptake or reduce their breakdown can be used to treat depressive disorders.

Table 9.1 Summary of hypotheses about mental disorders based on drug action

Drug	Effect	Action	Hypothesis
Phenothiazines	Reduce schizophrenic symptoms	Dopamine receptor blockade	Overactivity of dopaminergic systems in schizophrenia
Amphetamine	Paranoid symptoms	Dopamine release	
Tricyclic antidepressants	Reduce depression	Inhibition of mono-amine reuptake	Decreased mono-amine function in depression
Mono-amine oxidase inhibitors	Reduce depression	Decreased metabolism of mono-amines	
Reserpine	Can cause depression	Depletion of mono-amines	
Benzodiazepines	Reduce anxiety	Enhanced GABAergic inhibition	Decreased GABAergic inhibition in anxiety

Positive correlations between the effectiveness of antidepressant drugs and the extent to which amine depletion is reversed appear to support the theory. However, no clear correlations have been found between depression and concentrations of catecholamine or indole-amine metabolites, and while some indole-amine precursors have antidepressant effects, some catecholamine precursors do not (for example L-dopa). Such theoretical difficulties have suggested that biogenic amine dysfunction is certainly involved in depression, but that the precise causal relationship remains in doubt.

Similar reasoning, based on the anxiety-reducing action of the benzodiazepine drugs, suggests that GABAergic (GABA = gamma-aminobutyric acid) inhibition is deficient in anxiety. Normal anxiety is thought to depend on the action of a brain system involving the hippocampus and related limbic structures. When active, this system stops ongoing behaviour, increases arousal and directs attention towards possible danger. Benzodiazepines (and alcohol) are known to facilitate the inhibitory action of the neurotransmitter GABA, so that it seems likely that GABAergic transmission is involved in the control of this anxiety system.

Both this evidence and findings of asymmetrical blood-flow in the parahippocampal region of patients having panic attacks suggest that defective GABAergic control and related overactivity of the anxiety system in the brain may be implicated in abnormal anxiety.

Life events and vulnerability factors

Social theories of emotional disorders stress the importance of significant events that trigger anxiety or depression, and social circumstances associated with vulnerability to such events (see Chapter 6). The majority of those who are depressed have recently experienced a loss of some kind (for example, a death in the family, or loss of a job), while anxious individuals are more likely to be concerned with a possible future danger (for example, a possibly serious illness, threatened break-up of a relationship). However, not all people who have experienced such losses or dangers become depressed or anxious (see Table 9.2).

Other factors must therefore influence the impact of a life event on a person, and these are termed vulnerability or protective factors. George Brown & Tirril Harris (1978) found that women are more likely to develop a depressive disorder if (a) they are of low socio-economic status, (b) they have several young children at

Table 9.2 Percentage of women experiencing mood disorder by type of event in the last year

Type of event	Depressed (17) (%)	Mixed (15) (%)	Anxiety (13) (%)	Non-case (119) (%)
Loss	65	80	15	10
Danger	47	73	77	12
Both	35	60	8	2

From Finlay-Jones & Brown (1981).

home, (c) they do not have a job outside the home, (d) they do not have a close and confiding relationship with another person and (e) their own mother died before they were 11 years old. If none of these vulnerability factors are present, a loss event will tend to have very little effect, while if all are present then a depressive disorder is far more likely.

If social circumstances determine the onset of mood disorders, then changes in neurotransmitter levels may accompany depression, but they could not be said to bring it about. However, life events and vulnerability factors do not provide a complete theory either; some other process must link the social influences with the neuro-physiological changes that undoubtedly occur in emotional disorders.

Cognitive behavioural theories

Current psychological theories suggest that anxiety and depression arise from cognitive and behavioural reactions that have been learned from earlier experiences. Behaviour resembling phobic or anxiety states can be induced in animals by conditioning (see Chapter 3). However, when unsignalled or unpredictable shock is given with no possibility of escape or avoidance the result is a state of learned helplessness in which the animal become passive and unresponsive to further punishment. If the animal is now trans-ferred to the normal avoidance-conditioning situation it will make no attempt to escape, even when this could be easily achieved. Such apparently helpless behaviour, together with the finding of low noradrenaline levels in the brains of these animals, has led some researchers to consider that human depression is acquired in an analogous way.

Unlike animals, humans can report their thoughts and clinical observations suggest that depressive disorders are characterised by stereotyped thoughts of helplessness and hopelessness, or in the case of anxiety states by thoughts of possible danger. More experimental studies have shown that depressed patients have a systematic bias in memory favouring the recall of unpleasant events. Anxious patients show a similar tendency, but in this case it favours the perception of possibly threatening aspects of their environment. Cognitive theories thus suggest that depression (or anxiety) may indeed be triggered by recent events, but that it may be the way in which these events are remembered or perceived that determines which individual becomes depressed (or anxious) and which does not.

Is integration possible?

Although expressed in very different terms, the above approaches are perhaps not quite as contradictory as they may appear. It has already been suggested that emotional disorders may result only when a particular type of life event is interpreted in a negative way by the individual concerned. It was also noted that the experience of uncontrollable punishment is known to lead to noradrenaline depletion in brain systems thought to be involved with reinforcement and punishment. Depressive disorders (and, with some variations, anxiety states also) may thus correspond to a temporary breakdown in the brain systems that control normal emotional behaviour. Figure 9.2 illustrates this multifactorial approach, and integrates psychological, social and neurophysiological evidence.

PSYCHOLOGICAL TREATMENT

Psychological methods in medical practice

All clinicians use psychological treatment methods in their everyday work, whether they realise it or not, whenever they try to educate, to reassure or reduce distress, or to change their patients' behaviour. No doctor has the option whether to use psychological treatment or not, but only whether to use it well or badly. However, the actual methods used tend to vary very widely, from 'common sense' to methods based on psychoanalysis, or techniques developed from more recent behavioural and cognitive research. To make the distinctions between these methods clearer, suppose the patient is a 30-year-old married man who has suddenly become sexually impotent. He is desperate to receive help, but no physical pathology can be

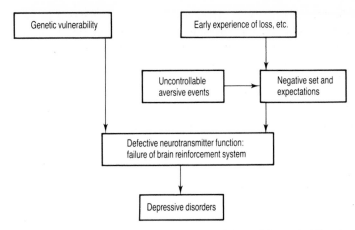

Fig. 9.2 Factors believed to be involved in the aetiology of depressive disorders, showing the chain of causation proposed by Akiskal & McKinney (1973).

discovered. Should you try to uncover the underlying causes of the problem by looking for unconscious sexual conflicts? Or should you attempt to reduce anxiety by relaxation and reassurance while encouraging a gradual return to sexual activity? Or should you try to change any misconceptions and worries about sex that may be on his mind? In the sections that follow, each of these approaches will be discussed in the light of the available evidence.

Dynamic psychotherapies

Based initially on psychoanalytic theory, these treatments assume that neurotic symptoms require the patient to become fully conscious of the historical origins underlying the present problem. Achieving this awareness (insight) requires patients to talk freely about their feelings in relation to the past, with minimum interference on the part of the therapist. Progress towards insight is guided by appropriate interpretations made by the therapist that rephrase what has gone before in psychoanalytic terms (for example, 'You feel guilty about sex because your wife reminds you in some ways of your mother').

Psychoanalytic treatments are notoriously lengthy and more recent variations of psychotherapy are briefer, or even time limited in advance. Brief psychotherapy differs from psychoanalysis in its focus on present feelings and current problems, avoiding lengthy explorations of the past. However, it is still considered to be non-directive, that is, the therapist may guide patients towards the expression of feelings, but never offers direct advice, and attempts instead to provide an accepting and non-judgemental setting.

Rather than psychoanalytic interpretations, therapists make more use of reflection, which is essentially a restatement of what the patient has just said to convey the feeling of being understood (for example, 'It seems as if you're afraid your wife may see you as a failure because of this problem').

Evaluation of psychotherapy

In 1952, Hans Eysenck published one of the most controversial papers in the history of psychology. He argued that there was no good evidence that dynamic psychotherapy helped patients at all, and that it might actually be doing them harm. It was possible for Eysenck to argue this because (a) some neurotic symptoms vary in severity or even disappear without special treatment (spontaneous remission), and (b) no controlled trial of psychotherapy had ever been carried out. The fact that some patients were said to improve following psychotherapy means nothing unless it can be shown that more such patients improved than would in a control group that did not receive any treatment.

Although Eysenck's paper was initially the subject of bitter dispute, it is now widely accepted that all psychological treatment in common usage should be scientifically evaluated. A controlled-treatment trial of psychotherapy implies that: (i) patients are randomly assigned to different treatment groups, (ii) groups are comparable in all important ways other than the type of treatment given, and (iii) outcome is assessed using objective measures of outcome (not just the therapist's opinion). Trials sometimes include a no-treatment control condition, such as a group of patients assigned to a treatment waiting list, although there are ethical and methodological objections to this. All treatments contain 'non-specific components' such as time and attention from clinicians, increased expectations of improvement and so on. Superiority of a treated over a non-treated group might thus reflect only the power of these non-specific factors. A non-specific control (or placebo) condition includes all these factors, but excludes the specific ingredients under test. A rigorous comparison of psycho-analytic treatment with an appropriate non-specific control has still not been carried out.

Behaviour therapy

Dissatisfaction with the failure to show that psychoanalytic treatment was objectively effective led eventually to the application of learning theory and methods to emotional disorders (see Chapter 3). In 1958 Joseph Wolpe described a new method of treating phobic anxiety based on counter conditioning, called *systematic desensitisation*. On the assumption that phobias were conditioned avoidance reactions, he first trained patients in muscle relaxation to inhibit anxiety, and then exposed them to a series of phobic stimuli or situations. The patient was asked to enter the least frightening situation, either in imagination or in reality, while remaining as relaxed as possible. As fear to the first stimulus declined, the patient was encouraged to move on to the next one and so on. Applying the same principles to impotence would thus require the patient to practice relaxation in situations of gradually increasing sexual intimacy.

Laboratory studies of desensitisation

Behavioural methods have been extensively tested using mild common fears, such as those of snakes or public speaking. In one study, volunteers were randomly assigned to brief treatment using desensitisation, dynamic psychotherapy, a non-specific placebo control, or no treatment, and the effects tested in a public-speaking situation before and after treatment. Both in terms of subjective report and in objective indices of anxiety, more subjects improved following desensitisation. Related studies have found that other types of learning such as real life practice with social reinforcement, or modelling followed by patient participation, has similar if not better results (see Fig. 9.3). The common factor underlying treatments found to be successful in these laboratory studies is that of progressive *exposure* to feared situations without avoidance.

Comparative clinical trials

Across a range of problems (phobias, obsessions, sexual problems etc.) evidence from controlled trials now shows that behavioural treatments are effective. Not all such treatments are based on desensitisation, or even exposure to feared situations. They may also involve acquiring new adaptive behaviours (e.g. social skills training) or the reduction of inappropriate behaviour (e.g. obsessional rituals).

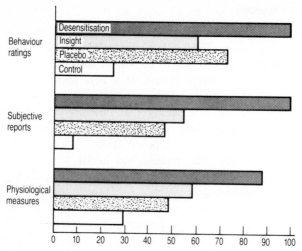

Fig. 9.3 Percentage of subjects showing reduction in behavioural, subjective and physiological indices of anxiety following systematic desensitization, insight psychotherapy, placebo or no treatment (From Paul G (1966) 'Insight versus desensitization in psychotherapy', Stanford University Press. Reproduced with permission.)

The question remains however; are these behavioural treatments more effective than dynamic psychotherapy? In a study reported by Sloane and his colleagues (1975), patients with anxiety and personality problems were randomly assigned to dynamic psychotherapy, behaviour therapy or a waiting-list control group. After 4 months of treatment and a 1-year follow-up period progress was reviewed by an interviewer who did not know what treatment (if any) had been received (Table 9.3). Overall, mean change in symptom severity was greatest following behaviour therapy, although psychotherapy patients also improved more than controls on the waiting list. However, while 93% of behaviour therapy patients showed at least some improvement, only 77% of dynamic therapy patients did so,

Table 9.3 Average complaint scores (scale 0–12) at pretreatment, post-treatment and follow-up

	Pre-treatment	Post-treatment	Follow-up (1 year)
Behavioural psychotherapy	8.8	4.5	3.8
Psychoanalytic therapy	9.1	5.3	4.9
Waiting-list control	8.8	6.5	5.5

From Sloane et al (1975).

which was no different from the rate achieved by the waiting-list control.

Cognitive therapy

In many disorders, such as depression, treatment such as behaviour therapy is difficult to apply. Patients typically resist behaviour change, since they view their situation as hopeless, and instead must be treated with drugs. However, research on cognitive processes has led to treatments aimed at changing thoughts as well as behaviour.

Therapists must first identify inappropriate negative thoughts (for example, 'All my life has been a failure') and help patients to question the accuracy of such beliefs (for example, 'Can you think of anything that seemed an achievement at the time?'). Once it is accepted that their thoughts are a distorted version of the truth, patients can be encouraged to reformulate them in a more realistic form (for example, 'Perhaps I have had some small successes in the past') and to try some behavioural 'experiments' to test predictions about the certainty of future failure. In this way, the distorted beliefs are systematically exposed to contradictory evidence, and as alternative ways of thinking are adopted so the depressed mood tends to improve. In a number of trials of this method (developed by the American psychiatrist Aaron Beck) cognitive therapy has been compared with antidepressant medication, and in each case found to be at least as effective. The fact that the psychological and pharmacologic . methods have similar effects provides some support for the integrated view of depression outlined earlier.

SEXUAL PROBLEMS AND TREATMENT

Sexual dysfunction and its treatment provides a convenient means of illustrating and bringing together some of the topics in this chapter. In men, common sexual dysfunctions include impotence (erectile failure) and premature ejaculation; in women they are vaginismus (involuntary and painful contraction of the vaginal muscles) and loss of sexual arousal. Although symptoms such as impotence can result from physical causes, their origins are more usually psychological. Vaginismus for example, is usually accompanied by fears of possible internal damage, and avoidance of sexual contact, typically dating from previous painful sexual experience. Impotence often begins with one or more erectile failures when the patient is tired or unwell, which are then viewed with alarm and evidence of failure. In both these disorders it is likely that earlier adverse experiences are relevant in creating psychological vulnerability, but that specific learning events trigger their onset, while alarming misconceptions serve to maintain or exacerbate the problem.

Sex therapy

Effective psychological treatment for sexual dysfunctions (developed by William Masters & Virginia Johnson) thus combines re-education with behavioural practice and methods of countering self-destructive thoughts. Couples are usually seen together and areas of sexual ignorance or misinformation are first rectified. A ban on attempts at intercourse is often imposed at this stage to reduce fear of further failure or pain, and instead the couple is requested to go through a series of touching and caressing exercises, only gradually returning to sexual activity as anxiety recedes and enjoyment returns.

Within this general framework, specific techniques are introduced to deal with each type of problem separately. In the case of vaginismus for example, a couple may be asked to insert a graded series of vaginal dilators under relaxed circumstances, in order to reduce the conditioned vaginal spasm. Once this has been achieved, intercourse may be resumed in a non-threatening way, with open discussion of feelings at each stage. Controlled studies of this combined method have shown it to be more effective than each of its separate component parts, that is, counselling, desensitisation, or behavioural instruction used alone.

FURTHER READING

Bradley B, Thompson C 1985 Psychological applications in psychiatry. Wiley, Chichester
Hawton K 1985 Sex therapy: a practical guide. Oxford University Press, New York
McGuffin P, Schanks M, Hodgson R 1984 The scientific principles of psychopathology. Academic Press, London

STUDY QUESTIONS

1. Summarise the evidence for genetic and environmental factors in emotional disorders.

2. What distinguishes the following conditions: generalised anxiety, agoraphobia, specific phobias, obsessional–compulsive neurosis, endogenous and reactive depression?
3. Discuss evidence for and against the amine theory of depression.
4. Summarise the psychoanalytic and learning-theory accounts of neurosis.
5. Describe the use of controlled trials to evaluate the effectiveness of psychological treatment.
6. Describe the usual causes and treatment of impotence.

10

Doctors and patients: communication and problem solving

COMMUNICATION IN MEDICAL SETTINGS

Visiting the doctor, or being treated in hospital, can be a bewildering and distressing experience for many people. There are several reasons why communication is an important aspect of health care, quite apart from the general humanitarian desire to reduce a patient's discomfort.

(a) *Diagnosis and decision making.* The patient provides much of the information on which a doctor makes a diagnosis. A good rapport is especially important when the doctor enquires about potentially embarrassing subjects, concerning perhaps sex or psychological symptoms. Frequently, patients present with a problem that they consider 'acceptable' when their real concerns lie elsewhere; if they are not treated with courtesy and consideration, the most important problem may never even be discussed.

(b) *Treatment and management.* Effective communication is essential to all forms of treatment. If drugs are given, the doctor must ensure that the patient understands the dosage, while in other forms of management the patient must again understand instructions and recognise the value of following them. Many treatments themselves affect quality of life (colostomy, mastectomy, etc.), and consultation with patients must go beyond the purely physical aspects of management.

(c) *Distress during medical procedures.* Surgery and other diagnostic procedures may arouse anticipatory fears and uncertainties which can be alleviated in part by providing patients with a framework of communication in which information and advice about coping can be transmitted effectively (see Chapter 6).

(d) *Patient satisfaction.* The degree to which patients are satisfied with care is strongly influenced by their relations with medical staff. Some surveys have shown that patients' satisfaction with a medical consultation is positively correlated with the likelihood that they will follow advice (see Chapter 11).

Table 10.1 Patients' satisfaction with communication

Patient group	Percentage of patients who are dissatisfied (median of studies)
General practice patients (3 studies)	35
Hospital in-patients (4 studies)	53
Psychiatric in-patients (9 hospitals)	39
Various patient groups in the USA (4 studies)	36

From Ley (1982).

Patient satisfaction with communication

A number of surveys of satisfaction with communication have been carried out, and Table 10.1 summarises results. A substantial proportion of patients are dissatisfied with communication in medical settings, while most are content with other aspects of care.

Many studies have attempted to identify the characteristics of patients who are not satisfied with communication in medical settings. No consistent relationships have been found with personality factors, the seriousness of the disease or the length of consultation. The common belief that communication would be improved if doctors had more time is not supported by the data; the way that time is used seems to be more important than total duration. Factors that have been found to relate to satisfaction with communication are discussed below.

Communication skills

There is an enormous variation in the quality and quantity of information elicited by different doctors, and this is affected both by diagnostic problem-solving abilities (see below) and by communication skills. For example, the initial impression in the consultation can affect attitudes to subsequent questioning, and many doctors begin the interaction poorly; they may be writing when the patient enters the room and not look up or greet the patient before asking questions. Other skills that are important include the mode of questioning. Many doctors are overdirective in their interview style, asking closed rather than open-ended questions, interrupting patients so that the problem or illness is not described clearly, and failing to pick up cues to unexpressed concerns. Patients also complain about the use of medical jargon and a brisk and business-like as opposed to friendly attitude.

Patients' beliefs and knowledge

Dissatisfaction with communication may arise from differences in the interpretation of clinical conditions. Most patients enter a consultation with their own opinions concerning the nature of their problem and the treatment that they expect. These beliefs may not coincide with the diagnosis and course of management suggested by the doctor. The patient may therefore leave the consultation with doubts about the doctor's understanding of the problem. One study of consultations in general practice showed that on subsequent interview, about one-quarter of patients were not convinced by the doctor's views on diagnosis, treatment or preventive action. Lack of commitment to the doctor's interpretation was more common in women, patients from ethnic minorities, the elderly or young children, and in patients seeing the doctor for the first time.

Korsch and her collaborators (1971) conducted a series of investigations on consultations in a walk-in emergency children's clinic in Los Angeles. Satisfaction with communication assessed at a follow-up interview was reduced when things that the patient's mother expected to happen did not take place, such as being given injections or X-rays, being given medicine, or being told the diagnosis and course of the illness.

Patients' interpretation of medical terms

The discrepancies between doctors' and patients' views may arise from incorrect or incomplete knowledge about bodily functioning. Multiple choice questionnaires on medical facts were completed by 234 out-patients in a study published in 1970, and wide variations in knowledge were observed. Two examples concerning the position of organs are illustrated in Figure 10.1. Definitions of common terms also varied. For example, while 100% of the doctors agreed that a palpitation was 'a feeling of the heart thumping inside the chest', only 52% of patients endorsed this view. Twenty-six per cent considered palpitation to mean 'a feeling of breathlessness', while 15% defined it as 'a feeling of fright and panic'. Clearly, it cannot be assumed that doctors and patients necessarily mean the same thing when using common medical terms. Even among doctors, there is sometimes disagreement about the meaning of terms.

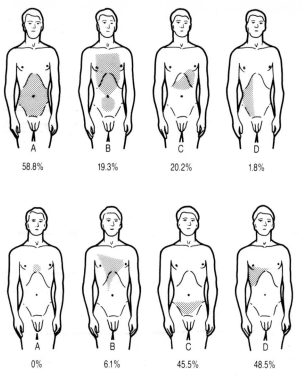

Fig. 10.1 The location of organs: outpatients were asked the location of the stomach (top panel) and liver (bottom panel). Doctors agreed that the correct locations were C (stomach) and D (liver). However, patients' responses were different, as can be seen from the percentages indicated. (From Boyle (1970), British Medical Journal (2). Reproduced with the permission of the editor.)

Provision of information

Another important factor affecting patients' satisfaction with communication is the amount of information that is provided. Many patients are dissatisfied with what they are told about the diagnosis, likely course and treatment of their condition, and feel that medical staff are unnecessarily secretive. Table 10.2 summarises results from a study of 100 surgical patients in a teaching hospital, showing the proportions of people dissatisfied with the amount of information they are given. Similarly, patients in convalescence frequently complain that they have not been told about what they can do at home. For instance, cardiac patients need to be advised about exercise, diet, whether they can engage in sexual activity or drive a car.

Table 10.2 Patients' satisfaction with information provided

Type of information	Percentage dissatisfied
How long investigations would take	23
Prior explanation of what to expect during the investigations	28
Explanations given during investigations	30
Why the tests were necessary	24
Results of the tests	38

From Reynolds (1978).

Sometimes patients are given information but fail to understand it. The British psychologist Philip Ley has investigated the intelligibility of written information typically provided in medical settings, using readability formulas that can be used to estimate the percentage of the population who would understand written material. He found that many leaflets concerning X-rays, cancer, health education and drug prescriptions are probably unintelligible to more than half the population. The use of medical jargon and technical terms may make information even harder to understand.

Why do patients not enquire more?

The obvious rejoinder to patients' complaints that they are not given information is to suggest that they should ask more questions. In fact, a number of studies have now shown that when patients do enquire their concerns are frequently ignored or brushed aside rather than being properly explored. In addition, patients are often diffident about asking for information, since the medical setting does not encourage such enquiries. Here is a quotation from a patient interviewed by sociologist Anne Cartwright (1964):

'I learned indirectly the names of the tablets I was having. I gathered it was an understood thing that you didn't ask the doctor — they would take it amiss if you did. I wouldn't have had the audacity to ask the sister in case of a snub. She might say 'It's none of your business to know what you're having'. I don't know how the sister or staff nurse would react if you asked them directly.'

These concerns of patients may be well founded. Vocal patients who always want to know about what is happening to them and refuse to take medications unless their purpose is explained may be classified as uncooperative.

Doctors' views of communication

Less is known about doctors' views of a successful consultation. However, a study by Cartwright (1976) suggests that general practitioners' views of a successful consultation differ markedly from those of patients. A number of factors related to doctors' satisfaction with consultations are summarised in Table 10.3. It can be seen that doctors tended to consider consultations very satisfactory if they were brief, if the patient asked few questions and did not talk too much, and if the consultation was confined to a single topic.

Table 10.3 Doctors' satisfaction with consultation

	Percentage of consultations described as 'very satisfactory'
Conversation time:	
Less than 5 minutes	46
5 minutes or longer	23
Proportion of conversation time during which the patient spoke:	
Less than 60%	46
60% or more	15
Number of questions asked by the patient:	
0 or 1	50
2 or 3	38
4 or more	24
Number of problems discussed:	
Less than 4	38
4 or more	21
All consultations	29

From Cartwright (1976).

Methods of improving communication

Methods of structuring information so as to enhance patients' recall have been detailed in Chapter 3, while the provision of information and coping strategies to surgical patients was outlined in Chapter 6. Other methods of improving communication in medical settings include the training of

Table 10.4 Recommendations concerning consultants

1. Find out what the patient's worries are. Do not confine yourself to gathering objective medical information.
2. Find out what the patient's expectations are. If they cannot be met, explain why.
3. Provide information about the diagnosis and cause of the illness.
4. Adopt a friendly rather than business-like attitude.
5. Avoid medical jargon.
6. Spend some time in conversation about non-medical topics.

From Korsch et al (1971).

communication skills in medical students. This usually involves small group sessions in which individual students or doctors interview real or simulated patients. The consultations are recorded on audio- or videotape, and the recordings are then replayed to the group so that specific points and deficits can be identified and discussed. Controlled trials indicate that these methods improve communication in terms of both consultation technique and the amount of data acquired to a significantly greater extent than the traditional apprenticeship method in which students observe 'experts' at work. Table 10.4 summarises recommendations about improving satisfaction with the communication aspect of consultations.

Increasing the intelligibility of written material by shortening and simplifying sentences may also have a positive effect on health care. For example, psychiatric patients often do not realise that antidepressant medications may take several days to exert their effects, and are sometimes uncertain about what to do once they have forgotten to take a tablet. An experiment was conducted in which patients receiving antidepressants or tranquillisers were given leaflets containing this information, written either in a very simple fashion or in the more difficult style that is typical of prescription leaflets. Table 10.5 summarises some of the results, which are expressed in terms of the percentage of pills which should have been taken. It can be seen that pill taking was improved by giving the easy leaflet, while adherence among patients given the difficult leaflet was no better than when no leaflet at all was provided.

Communicating bad news

There are special problems in telling patients that they suffer from a serious and possibly irreversible illness. Surveys of the general

Table 10.5 Pill taking and comprehensibility of information

	Adherence to medication (%)		
	No leaflet	Difficult leaflet	Easy leaflet
Patients receiving:			
Antidepressants	83.8	85.5	97.0
Tranquillisers	85.4	85.1	94.2

From Ley (1976).

population indicate that the vast majority of people say that they would want to be told if they had a fatal illness. Studies of patients with terminal cancer are less clear, but indicate that well over half wish to be informed of the diagnosis, while many others may suspect that they are dying even without being explicitly told. The desire of patients to know is even stronger in progressive disorders such as multiple sclerosis. Patients state that being given a diagnosis enables them to make plans while they are still fit, and may also provide an explanation for worrying symptoms.

Many doctors are reluctant to inform patients about terminal disease until a late stage. The reasons generally given are that telling patients may cause harm since patients will give up hope, or that the prognosis is uncertain so that it is unfair to inform patients of more pessimistic expectations. These reasons are not very convincing; more harm may be done by damaging the doctor–patient relationship through false reassurance, and most patients do not respond to knowledge that they are dying by giving up hope. The lack of an accurate prognosis does not prevent physicians from making a working judgement.

It is likely that doctors' reluctance to inform patients is related to the difficulty of breaking bad news. Doctors may have a number of anxieties about this situation, including fear of being blamed for their failure to make patients better, fear of eliciting serious emotional responses, and difficulties that they themselves have in expressing sympathy and displaying emotion, since these go against the professional image of the doctor as caring but objective.

Methods of improving doctors' skills at breaking bad news have primarily involved seminar groups and the use of videotaped or simulated patients, so that students learn to handle difficult emotional situations, how to admit their ignorance to patients and other problems.

PROBLEM SOLVING AND DIAGNOSIS

Diagnosis is a form of problem solving, so our understanding of problem solving in general is relevant to medical care. One view of problem solving is that the person accumulates all available information concerning a problem before reaching a decision. In clinical terms, the doctor would ask all relevant questions and conduct all possible tests appropriate for the symptoms before making a tentative diagnosis. Alternatively, problem solving has been seen as analogous to computer functioning, with a solution being attained through a series of logical steps, in which all possible alternatives are systematically narrowed down.

In practice, people frequently short-circuit these logical problem-solving procedures, and use *heuristics* to help in decision making. Heuristics are rules of thumb, or simplified decision strategies that are conventionally followed in particular circumstances. They are typically based on such things as previous experience with similar problems. Thus a doctor seeing a particular type of rash on the skin is likely to think about how it resembles the rashes of previous patients. This leads to the early generation of a hypothesis which can be tested. Thus the question of diagnosis rapidly changes from being an open-ended problem with an indefinite number of possible

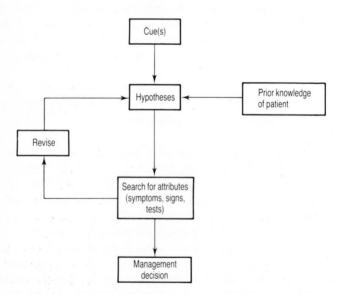

Fig. 10.2 Stages in diagnostic problem solving. (From McWhinney, 'Problem solving and decision making', Proceedings of the Royal Society of Medicine. Oxford University Press, 1972. Reprinted with permission.)

solutions to a situation in which a specific possibility is tested. If this fails, another hypothesis is sought, and so on. The process is outlined in Figure 10.2.

Several factors emerge from this general model of problem solving that are relevant to the diagnostic process:

(a) A commonly used heuristic in medical decision making is known as *representativeness*. That is, a specific instance (say a symptom) is likely to be taken as evidence of a category (say a disease) to the extent that it is typical or representative of symptoms occurring in that disease category. While useful, this rule of thumb ignores the possibility that the same symptom may also occur (even if less typically) in other conditions which may be numerically more common (that is, have a higher *base rate*).

Suppose a certain form of cancer has a prevalence of 1 in 1000 people. A screening test having a 95% detection accuracy and a 5% false positive rate for this form of cancer shows that you have the disease. In the absence of any other symptoms or signs, what are the chances that you have the cancer? Try answering before you continue.

If your answer was 95% — think again. The base rate for the cancer means that for every 1000 people tested 1 true case is detected (95% certainty), while the other 999 non-cases would yield almost 50 false positives (5% of 999). So your chances of having cancer are really 1 in 50, or 2%. Because a positive result is typical for true cancer cases, it is easy to overlook the fact that 'unrepresentative' false positives are much more common among the whole population.

(b) Another heuristic that may be important in medical decision making is the *availability bias*. People tend to judge an event as likely or frequent if it is easy to imagine or to recall. For example, because dramatic and sensational types of death (such as murder and natural disasters) are so frequently discussed in conversation and in the media, their likelihood tends to be overestimated. In the diagnostic context, a doctor who has recently encountered a rare cause of symptoms may diagnose the problem again, even though other causes are statistically much more likely.

(c) A common feature in problem solving is that tests are generated that seek to confirm particular hypotheses. The more confirmatory evidence that is obtained, the firmer the conclusion appears to be. However, positive tests are sometimes less useful than negative tests, since the latter are important in ruling out alternative explanations. There is a danger that the diagnosis is not properly established since no attempts are made to disconfirm it.

Studies of diagnostic interviews indicate that few questions are asked by doctors that are designed to rule out the provisional interpretation that has been made.

(d) Specialist clinicians tend to think in terms of the particular symptoms and causes studied in their own discipline. Thus an allergist will look for allergic causes, a neurologically orientated psychiatrist may look for signs of brain damage, while a socially orientated psychiatrist may seek the cause of the patient's problems in the social environment. When a patient has been referred to a specialist, the problem may then be seen purely in the context of this specialty. The danger of the narrow view is that illnesses may remain undiagnosed because the doctor treating the patient does not consider problems outside his or her specialty.

Psychological problems in medical patients

Studies of patients on medical and surgical wards indicate that a substantial proportion have psychological disturbances of a sufficient intensity to warrant specialist help. For example, one survey of patients on medical wards showed that 23% had serious affective disorders, chiefly depression. Rates of psychological problems among surgical patients may be even higher. Less than half of these psychological problems are detected or treated appropriately by the staff. Typically, referral to a psychiatrist is made when patients are uncooperative and complaining, but those depressed people who are quiet and docile may not be given psychological help. The reverse may be the case as well; one study of psychiatric in-patients showed that marked physical illnesses were present in 33%, but only half of these illnesses had been recognised.

Decisions about patient management

Doctors are frequently faced with decisions about which course of action to take. For example, should an antihypertensive drug be used to reduce moderately elevated blood-pressure, given that side-effects may occur, and that the risk of myocardial infarction or stroke is only slightly elevated? Or should breast cancer be treated with surgery or chemotherapy? Such decisions are taken on the basis of clinical judgement, plus an evaluation of therapeutic trials and the statistics on mortality and morbidity.

However, it has been found that decision making of this type is not entirely systematic and objective. Psychologists Kahneman &

Tversky have shown that decisions are influenced by the ways in which problems are presented. These *framing* effects can be illustrated in the following problem, in which a large group of radiologists were asked about whether they would prefer surgery or radiation as a treatment for lung cancer (McNeil et al 1982). Surgery has a greater initial mortality associated with the operation itself, but the subsequent death rate is lower. The relevant statistics were presented in one of two possible ways:

1. 'Of 100 people having surgery, 10 will die during treatment, 32 will have died by 1 year, and 66 will have died by 5 years. Of 100 people having radiation therapy, none will die during treatment, 23 will die by 1 year, and 78 will die by 5 years'.

2. 'Of 100 people having surgery, 90 will survive treatment, 68 will survive at 1 year, and 34 will survive for 5 years. Of 100 people having radiation therapy, all will survive treatment, 77 will survive at 1 year, and 22 will survive for 5 years.'

It can be seen that these are the same statistics, presented in terms either of death or survival. When physicians were presented with the statistics in terms of death rates, 50% chose radiation and 50% chose surgery. But of those given the statistics in terms of survival, only 16% preferred radiation. It seems as if the doctors were much more strongly influenced by the treatment mortality when statistics were presented in terms of death rates, and by the poorer long term outcome following radiation when statistics were presented in terms of survival.

FURTHER READING

Kahneman D, Tversky A 1984 Choices, values and frames. American Psychologist 39: 341–350
Ley P 1982 Chapter 14 in: Eiser J R (ed.) Social psychology and behavioral medicine. Wiley, Chichester
Maguire P 1984 Chapter 5 in: Steptoe A, Mathews A (eds.) Health care and human behaviour. Academic Press, London

STUDY QUESTIONS

1. What factors influence patient satisfaction with communications?
2. What problems are experienced by patients who wish to know more about their condition?
3. How can doctor–patient communication be improved?
4. What methods can be used to train doctors in communicating with patients?
5. What are heuristics, and how do they influence medical decision making?
6. Outline the importance of framing effects in decision making.

11

Health promotion: changing attitudes and behaviour

Much of medical practice consists of changing patients' behaviour. Drugs may be prescribed to be taken at particular times of day, and for a stated duration. A special diet or exercise regimen may be recommended. Patients may be asked to stop doing something, such as smoking or drinking alcohol. Each of these represents an attempt to change behaviours. Doctors often believe that patients will naturally follow advice given for their own good, although research on learning (see Chapter 3) suggests otherwise. Changes in behaviour are unlikely to occur if patients simply do not understand or remember the advice they have been given, and any changes achieved may not persist if they are not reinforced.

The extent to which patients follow the medical advice they have been given is usually termed *compliance*, or treatment *adherence*. Compliance is frequently thought to depend on the beliefs or attitudes of patients towards medical advice. If patients do not accept the same assumptions as their doctors, the advice given may be seen as pointless and may be rejected (see Chapter 10). For example, the middle-aged man who leaves the surgery still believing his angina to be a form of indigestion is not likely to persist in taking anti-anginal medication. However, even when patients share the assumptions and attitudes of their doctors, they may still fail to change their behaviour. Clearly, no matter how accurate the diagnosis and recommendations for treatment, the doctor's effectiveness is still crucially dependent on the extent to which patients adhere to the advice they have been given. As will be seen, this is far from being a trivial problem.

THE EXTENT OF NON-COMPLIANCE

Various methods can be used to measure the extent of adherence to treatment. Most simply, patients may be asked to report on how many pills (for example) they have taken, and this can be compared

152

with the number recommended. More accuracy may be gained by counting any pills remaining, or by using a biochemical marker to detect the presence of drugs in blood or urine. Not surprisingly, estimates of adherence tend to be higher when they are based on patients' reports than when they are based on objective methods.

If patients are found to have followed advice with an accuracy of 80% or more (e.g. 80% of prescribed pills taken at approximately the right time), they are usually considered to be compliant. Using this arbitrary criterion, Table 11.1 shows typical levels of adherence gathered over many independent studies. It can be seen that:

1. Overall compliance is low, with only a little over half of all patients adhering to their treatment régime.
2. Even with potentially dangerous physical disease (e.g. diabetes or tuberculosis) patients do not adhere significantly better.
3. Psychiatric patients do not differ markedly from other patients in adherence rates.
4. The range of adherence found in different studies is very wide, from less than 10% to more than 90%.

It is evident that non-compliance is widespread, and that neither diagnosis nor severity is a reliable guide. Some other factors must be responsible for the striking variation found in compliance rates.

Table 11.1 Percentage of patients who were found to adhere to treatment advice

Type of advice	Number of studies	Range (%)	Mean (%)
TB drugs	20	92–24	62
Psychotropics	9	89–49	61
Antibiotics	8	89–8	51
Other drugs	12	81–13	51
Diet	11	80–16	51
Other advice	8	70–21	45
Total	68	92–8	56

Adapted from Ley (1977).

Doctors' estimates of non-compliance

It would obviously be helpful if doctors could predict which of their patients were likely to prove non-compliant. To study this, in-patients being treated for ulcers were given instructions on when to take antacid medication, and their consumption was observed unobtrusively by nurses. Doctors were asked to predict the extent of adherence to be expected from their own patients, and these estimates were then compared with the actual observations. In general, doctors' estimates of compliance were over-optimistic (the estimated compliance was 70%, the actual was 46%). More importantly, there was no significant correlation between the estimates made for each patient and that patient's level of compliance; that is, the doctor's accuracy for individual patients was essentially zero. Subsequent research has shown that there are no obvious personality characteristics associated with failure to comply. The reasons for individual differences in adherence must be sought elsewhere.

DETERMINANTS OF PATIENT COMPLIANCE

Effect of clinical context

Some important influences on compliance arise within the doctor–patient relationship (see Table 11.2). Close medical supervision tends to result in higher adherence, so that estimated compliance in one study was 80% for in-patients, compared with 60% for out-patients. However, irrespective of setting, patients who express high rather than low satisfaction following a medical consultation are more likely to follow advice (see Chapter 10 for the factors associated with patient satisfaction). As might be expected, factors that tend to undermine a good doctor–patient relationship, or to reduce patient satisfaction, result in relatively low rates of compliance. Such factors include long waiting times, and having to see different doctors at each visit. In sum, if doctor–patient contact satisfies the patient's psychological and social needs, then otherwise poor rates of adherence will be significantly improved. A good doctor–patient relationship is therefore not just desirable: it is essential for the effective practice of medicine.

Effect of treatment régimes

If treatment régimes involve no benefit that is obvious to the patient, or have disagreeable consequences such as drug side-effects, then compliance rates tend to drop. Conversely, if medication has immediate beneficial results, adherence is reinforced and tends to be higher. Taking medication involves relatively little change in behaviour, but other medical advice may require more radical changes in lifestyle. A hypertensive patient might be required to change his or her diet and to stop smoking, as well as

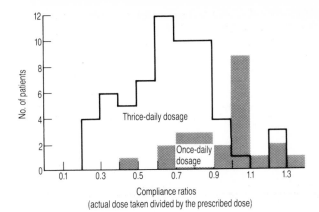

Fig. 11.1 Degree of adherence to medication requirements according to whether the same dose was taken in a once daily form, or divided into three (From Porter (1969) 'Drug defaulting in general practice', British Medical Journal. Reproduced with the permission of the editor.)

to take pills. In general, the more behavioural the change that is required, and the more aversive the consequences of treatment, the lower is the compliance rate.

Easy versus complex regimes

In one clinical study, 86 pregnant women were prescribed an iron preparation. Most were given the usual form that had to be taken three times a day. However, 24 women were experimentally assigned to a new preparation that could be taken just once daily. The results of this study (shown in Fig. 11.1) revealed a surprisingly large effect, with compliance being much better in the group taking the once-daily preparation. Compliance in the larger group taking three doses a day averaged about 65%, while the mean for the once-daily group was around 95% (compliance ratios above 1.0 show that a few women took more than was recommended). This study shows that apparently quite trivial differences in the ease of following a treatment régime can make quite dramatic differences to compliance rates.

Effect of social conditions

Many studies have failed to find any evidence that compliance depends on socio-economic status. However, a selection bias might obscure any real differences, since many people in the community experience symptoms of illness without their ever coming to the

Table 11.2 Summary of main factors influencing adherence

Increase adherence	Decrease adherence
High satisfaction with consultation	Poor doctor–patient relationship.
Patient believes treatment is important	Complicated treatment regimen
	Unpleasant side-effects
Observable benefit from treatment	Change in lifestyle required
Social support available	

attention of their doctor (the 'clinical iceberg'). This is believed to be particularly marked in lower socio-economic groups, since despite their greater absolute use of health resources they do not take up as much medical time as would be expected given their much higher morbidity rate. Thus it appears that lower socio-economic status is associated with relatively lower attendance and use of medical resources, making true adherence rate in this group difficult to estimate.

Only one clear finding of social background influences has been reported. Patients who are socially isolated tend to adhere to advice less than those with stable family or other forms of social support. Although the reasons for this effect are not clear, it seems likely that reminders and reinforcement from others to follow medical advice is one of the important influences underlying many of the correlations with compliance (Table 11.2).

ATTITUDES AND BEHAVIOUR

Attitudes are general and stable dispositions to feel favourably or unfavourably towards certain ideas, actions or groups. Such things as political preferences, racial prejudice or views about the medical profession are all examples of *attitudes*. Since it is often assumed that people will behave in a manner consistent with their attitudes, those that concern health matters may be important in compliance and disease prevention. A negative attitude towards smoking for example, might lead to reduction in cigarette consumption and in related lung diseases. Clearly it is preferable to prevent behaviours that cause ill health (*health promotion*) rather than to treat disorders after they have occurred. For this reason, it is important to understand how attitudes are formed, and to what extent attitude change produces a corresponding change in behaviour.

Attitude formation and change

Many fundamental attitudes are influenced less by rational choice than by emotional learning experiences. Exposure to the beliefs held by influential models help to shape attitudes in early life (see Chapter 3). Prejudice tends to arise when exposure to alternative views or models is limited or absent. Without necessarily being aware of the learning process, we each acquire a particular set of *social norms*, that is, standards of what is normal and socially acceptable. Deviations from such social norms meet with social disapproval or punishment. Although attitudes and social norms can sometimes be changed by rational argument or persuasion, experiments show that most are quite resistant to such methods. Change often requires regular exposure to alternative views and social pressure from other people whose approval is valued.

Attitudes towards breast-feeding

During pregnancy the behaviour of expectant mothers typically conforms to the expectations of the local community, especially their close relatives and friends, rather than to professional medical advice. Thus the eating, drinking and smoking habits of pregnant women tend to conform to social norms, even when these go against medical opinion. In some cases, these norms vary across time and social class. Breast feeding fell from favour in higher socio-economic groups at a time when it was seen as old fashioned, and the preference for bottle feeding spread slowly to other classes. The present view that breast feeding is medically and psychologically desirable has been accompanied by a gradual swing away from bottle feeding, again led by higher socio-economic groups, with other sections of society tending to change more slowly.

How do attitudes affect behaviour?

Contrary to what one might hope, the relationship between attitudes and behaviour is not always a simple one. Most smokers disapprove of the habit and say they wish to stop, while still continuing to smoke. Equally, many who approve of regular dental check-ups fail to visit the dentist themselves. Part of the apparent discrepancy is illusory: it depends on how attitudes are measured. Hence, smokers may achieve consistency between attitudes and behaviour by agreeing that they intend to stop, but not right now.

Their attitude remains that of general disapproval for smoking, but this applies to their long term rather than their immediate plans. However, to some extent the discrepancy is real, since a favourable attitude towards stopping is opposed by knowledge of the obstacles that will be encountered, such as withdrawal effects. To influence behaviour, attitude change must focus on immediate intentions rather than just general approval or disapproval.

PREVENTIVE HEALTH BEHAVIOUR

Prevention of heart disease

A number of recent studies have suggested that attitude change can help prevent diseases that are related to high risk behaviours. The World Health Organisation study of coronary heart disease (CHD) prevention involves educating large groups of healthy men about risk factors in CHD — for example, about diet, exercise and smoking habits. Results show that education alone is not always successful at modifying these risk behaviours, but in those who did reduce their weight, plasma cholesterol and blood-pressure deaths from CHD were significantly decreased. This was the case in Belgium, where deaths from CHD (per 10 000) were reduced from 139 in the control group to 95 in the instructed group, a reduction of 21%. Other evidence, based on smaller but more intensively studied samples, shows that the change in risk factors is more persistent if health education is combined with advice and practice in specific methods of changing behaviour. In one American study, plasma cholesterol levels had decreased by 45 mg/100 ml on follow-up by behaviourally treated patients, compared with 17 mg/100 ml for those who had been given only medical advice.

Persuasion via fear arousal

Attempts to change health-related attitudes have often involved materials intended to arouse fear of the consequences of non-compliance. Recent advertising campaigns aimed at preventing experimentation with drugs, for example, have tried to depict the consequences of abuse in a horrific way. Experiments comparing high-fear-arousing with low-fear-arousing films have shown that the more horrific films sometimes produce more attitude change, but that these differences are often short lived. In the long term, the anxiety induced by very horrific material may be reduced by rejecting it as exaggerated, or not applicable to the individual concerned. Information conveying a realistic picture of health risks tends to produce less immediate attitude change, but one that endures longer than that following excessively horrific presentations.

Fear arousal and behavioural change

Even when attitudes are altered by fear arousal, behaviour may not always follow suit. The reasons for this can be made clearer by considering the results of experiments that examine the interaction of fear arousal and instructions designed to facilitate behaviour change. In one study, students were advised to obtain tetanus injections, and were allocated at random to either a high or a low fear message. Each of these two groups was further subdivided, with half being given additional instructions concerned with how to find the clinic, and how to fit in a visit with their daily routine. As expected, the high fear message changed attitudes more, but in the absence of these additional behavioural instructions hardly any subjects actually obtained injections. Behavioural instructions alone or in combination with the low fear message were equally ineffective. The only significant number of subjects (30%) who attended for injections were those who had both the high fear message and behavioural instructions together.

The explanation for these findings may be that people tend to seek ways of reducing the fear aroused by threatening information. In the absence of behavioural solutions, they will either reject the message as inapplicable to them or simply feel helpless. If an effective and available behavioural solution is offered, however, many will accept and act on it.

In another study, smokers were given information implying either a very high or relatively low risk of cancer, and additional information which appeared to show either that stopping smoking would reduce this risk very considerably, or that it would have only a slight effect. Those receiving the high fear message showed the most evidence of a wish to stop smoking, but only if they also believed that this would substantially reduce their risk. High fear subjects who believed that stopping would have little effect actually showed less intention to stop than did the low fear subjects.

Combining information on risk and behaviour

The evidence just cited implies that patients at risk for a disease are best helped by being given a realistically (but not excessively) frightening picture of the consequences of not following medical advice, together with very explicit behavioural instructions on how the risk can be reduced. If such instructions are not given, or they are seen by the patient as ineffective or too difficult to achieve, then it is likely that patients may reject the message and react against it rather than comply. Adherence may also be weakened if the recommended action is not given at the same time as the warning message.

In one study of fear arousal, obese patients who had been advised to lose weight were allocated to one of three groups. All three groups received the same alarming message about the dangers of obesity, and were given detailed recommendations about how they could lose weight. However, the first group had the fear-arousing message first followed immediately by the recommendations, the second was given the same information in reverse order, while the third had a substantial delay period between the two sets of instructions. Figure 11.2 shows that the amount of weight lost subsequently was considerably less in the patients who had experienced a delay between the fear-inducing message and the behavioural instructions. Presumably the motivating influence of the fear induction in these patients had been dissipated rather than than being channelled effectively into behavioural intentions.

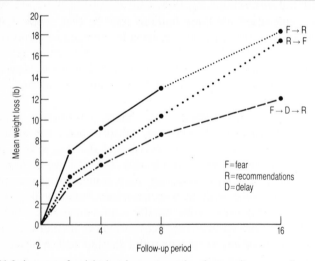

Fig. 11.2 Amount of weight lost in treatment by obese patients according to the order in which they had been given a fear-arousing message and recommendations about how to lose weight (From 'The effects of fear arousal, fear perception, fear exposure and sidedness on compliance with dietary instructions', Skilbeck et al, European Journal of Social Psychology. Copyright 1972, John Wiley and Sons Limited. Reproduced by permission of John Wiley and Sons Limited.)

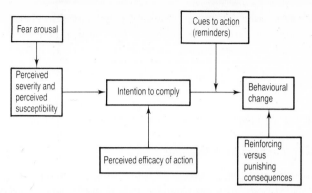

Fig. 11.3 Schematic representation of the health belief model, showing the direction of influence exerted by different psychological variables on behavioural change.

The health belief model

Beliefs about the likelihood of contracting a particular disease, and the severity of its effects, vary widely from person to person. The health belief model (see Fig. 11.3) is a rough description of the ways in which individual beliefs may facilitate or hinder health-related behaviours such as treatment adherence. Research shows that an individual's feelings and perceptions of susceptibility to a disease, and its probable effects, together serve to promote behaviour that the person believes will be effective in avoiding it. For example, if cigarette smokers perceive that their personal chances of contracting lung disease are high, and that lung disease would be unpleasant and dangerous, then the motivation for stopping smoking would be increased. Note that it is the smoker's beliefs about personal vulnerability that are involved, rather than medical opinion or knowledge of official statistics applying to others. Effective fear-evoking messages are thought to act by raising an individual's sense of vulnerability, and thus motivation to change.

The health belief model also suggests that individuals will only attempt to change their own behaviour if they believe that clear benefits will result, that is, the action must be seen as effective in reducing personal risk. However, the effects of such positive intentions to comply or change behaviour will also depend on environmental influences. Some, such as reminders of the desired actions or positive social reinforcement for them, will facilitate actual behavioural change. Others, such as apparent obstacles or temporary unpleasant consequences (e.g. side-effects of medication, or weight gain after stopping smoking), will prevent behavioural change despite positive motivation. The health belief model is summarised in diagrammatic form in Figure 11.3. Psychological variables are shown in boxes, linked by arrows indicating the supposed direction of influence.

HEALTH PROMOTION AND BEHAVIOUR CHANGE

Increasing adherence behaviour

Approaching clinical problems of adherence or prevention from a behavioural point of view suggests that changing beliefs and attitudes is a necessary first step, but will probably not be sufficient. In a study of 5000 male steel-workers carried out in Canada, measurement of blood-pressure showed that about 250 of the men were clinically hypertensive. These men were all offered medication, but in addition half were also given special instruction about the risks associated with high blood-pressure. Six months later less than half were still taking medication, and there was no significant difference in compliance or blood-pressure between the instructed and uninstructed groups. It was therefore decided to try again by assigning half of all those who had received instructions without benefit to a behavioural régime that consisted of the following components:

(a) Each patient was interviewed to identify daily habits and an agreement reached about a convenient schedule for taking hypotensive medication.

(b) Each was also loaned a home blood-pressure cuff and stethoscope, and asked to chart his blood-pressure together with medication taken.

(c) Patients were briefly interviewed every few weeks to review the charts and to encourage adequate compliance together with blood-pressure decreases.

As can be seen in Figure 11.4, this apparently simple programme showed significant benefits over and above education alone. Compliance had increased to 80% on 6 months' follow-up, compared with 40% for the control patients, and blood-pressure fell in a corresponding way. The behavioural approach used in this and other studies can be summarised by the following four steps:

1. Educate patients about health risks and the need for treatment.

2. Tailor the required treatment to the patient's existing habits.

3. Instruct patients to monitor the target behaviour and symptoms themselves.

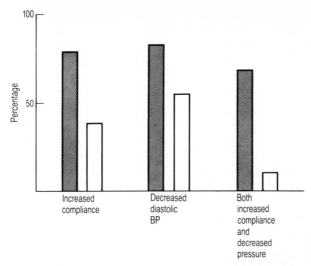

Fig. 11.4 Percentage of patients showing increased medication adherence and decreased blood-pressure over a 6-month period (shaded bars represent behaviourally treated patients and open bars represent controls). Mean compliance rose by 21% in the experimental group, and fell by 2% in the control group (From Haynes et al (1976) 'Improvement of medication compliance in uncontrolled hypertension', The Lancet. Reproduced with permission.)

4. Provide systematic social reinforcement for changes in the desired direction.

The problem of cigarette smoking

Smoking is a well-known behavioural health risk, so it is not surprising that it has been the focus of a great deal of research on cessation and prevention. Recent studies have shown that both psychological methods and the use of nicotine substitutes (such as nicotine-containing chewing gum) have significant effects. However, the effectiveness of nicotine gum depends crucially on whether it is used alone or in the right psychological context. Given alone it has very little impact, but when given in combination with psychological counselling up to 30% of smokers will stop completely. Nevertheless, a few become dependent on the gum itself, and many others stop smoking for a while only to relapse within a few months. Bearing in mind that only a tiny minority of smokers can receive specialised help on an individual basis, it is obvious that clinical treatment of dependent smokers offers no solution to the main problem.

Mass control can be approached in two ways: via widespread advertising and the use of other media resources, or by intensive preventive efforts at the stage before smoking begins (usually between 10 and 12 years of age). Although smoking rates are slowly falling in the UK, health warnings on advertisements or cigarette packets appear to have little impact on the majority of heavy smokers, as might be expected from the earlier discussion of behavioural change. A larger impact would probably follow a campaign which replaced cigarette advertising with fear-invoking messages combined with easy access to self-help advice and other financial incentives to stop.

Prevention of smoking in children

The more important question of primary prevention in children has been comparatively neglected. Those studies that have been carried out suggest that social pressure from same-age peers, and the modelling effect of high status older children and adults, are the most important factors involved in accepting the first few cigarettes. Undermining these influences by providing alternative high status models who refuse to accept cigarettes, and identifying smoking as childish rather than mature behaviour, may begin to reduce the numbers of children who take up smoking.

One such study in Oslo compared the smoking rates in 500 school children aged 10–15 years after half of them had met in groups aimed at discouraging smoking. Each group had a student leader, chosen to be a slightly older and attractive non-smoker. Group meetings involved discussion of social pressures to smoke and how to resist it, as well as the social and health disadvantages of smoking. At the end of the programme, 17% of the instructed children were smoking, but this compared with 27% of the controls, a significant difference.

FURTHER READING

Becker M H, Rosenstock I M 1984 Chapter 6 in: Steptoe A, Mathews A (eds) Health care and human behaviour. Academic Press, London
Di Matteo R, Di Nicola D D 1982 Achieving patient compliance. Pergamon Press, New York
Ley P 1977 Chapter 2 in: Rachman S J (ed) Contributions to medical psychology. Pergamon Press, Oxford

STUDY QUESTIONS

1. List the factors responsible for low rates of treatment adherence.
2. What are 'attitudes' and how are they formed?
3. Does the arousal of fear help to change attitudes?
4. Describe the 'health belief model'.
5. Construct a clinical management plan for a diabetic patient who neglects medical advice, and has poor insulin control.
6. How do you account for the persistence of smoking in people who have been told about the health risks?

References

Akiskal H, McKinney W 1973 Depressive disorders: toward a unified hypothesis. Science 182: 20–29

Atkinson R, Shiffrin R 1971 The control of short-term memory. Scientific American 224: 82–90

Balagura S, Hoebel B G 1967 Self-stimulation of the hypothalamic 'feeding-reward system' modified by insulin and glucagon. Physiology and Behavior 2: 337–340

Bandura A, Blanchard E, Ritter B 1969 The relative efficacy of desensitization and modelling approaches for inducing behavioral, affective and attitudinal changes. Journal of Personality and Social Psychology 13: 173–179

Bower T G R 1982 Development in infancy (2nd edn). W H Freeman, San Francisco

Boyle C M 1970 Difference between patients' and doctors' interpretation of some common medical terms. British Medical Journal 2: 286–289

Brown G W, Harris T 1978 Social origins of depression. Tavistock, London

Carmichael L, Hogan H, Walter A 1932 An experimental study of the effect of language on the reproduction of visually perceived form. Journal of Experimental Psychology 15: 73–86

Carter N 1980 Development and growth and ageing. Croom Helm, Beckenham

Cartwright A 1964 Human relations and hospital care. Routledge & Kegan Paul, London

Cartwright A 1976 What goes on in the general practitioner's surgery? In: Acheson A M, Aird L (eds) Seminars in community medicine Vol. 1: Sociology. Oxford University Press, London

Douglas J W B 1975 Early hospital admissions and later disturbances of behaviour and learning. Developmental Medicine and Child Neurology 17: 456–480

Egbert L, Battit G, Welch C, Barlett M 1964 Reduction of post-operative pain by encouragement and instruction of patients. New England Journal of Medicine 270: 825–827

Eysenck H J 1952 The effects of psychotherapy: an evaluation. Journal of Consulting Psychology 16: 319–324

Eysenck H J 1970 The structure of personality. Methuen, London

Eysenck H J, Wilson G (eds) 1976 A textbook of human psychology. MTP, Lancaster p 137

Fenz W D 1972 In: Sarason I G, Spielberger C D (eds) Stress and anxiety. Hemisphere, Washington D C p 320

Finlay-Jones R, Brown G 1981 Types of stressful life events and the onset of anxiety and depressive disorders. Psychological Medicine 11: 803–815

Fischer K, Lazerson A 1984 Human development. W H Freeman, Oxford

Fordyce W 1976 Behavioral methods in chronic pain and illness. C V Mosby, St Louis

Gebhard P, Johnson A 1979 The Kinsey data. Saunders, Philadelphia

Gilling D, Brightwell R 1982 The human brain. Orbis, London

Haynes B, Sackett D, Gibson E, Taylor W, Hackett B, Roberts R, Johnson A 1976 Improvement in medication compliance in uncontrolled hypertension. Lancet i: 1265–1976

Henry J P, Stephens P M, Santisteban G A 1975 A model of psychosocial hypertension showing reversibility and progression of cardiovascular complications. Circulation Research 36: 156–164

Jensen A R 1973 Educability and group differences. Harper and Row, New York

Korsch B, Freeman B, Negrete V 1971 Practical implications of doctor–patient interactions: analysis for pediatric practice. American Journal of Diseases of Children 121: 110–114

Lader M H, Wing L 1966 Physiological measures, sedative drugs, and morbid anxiety. Oxford University Press, London

Lazarus R S, Opton E M, Nomikos R S, Rankin N O 1965 The principle of short-circuiting of threat: further evidence. Journal of Personality 33: 622–635

Levitt R A 1981 Physiological psychology. Holt, Rinehart and Winston, New York, pp 215, 265, 275

Ley P 1976 Towards better doctor-patient communication. In: Bennett A E (ed) Communications between doctors and patients. Oxford University Press, London

Ley P 1977 Psychological studies of doctor-patient communication. In: Rachman S (ed) Contributions to medical psychology Vol. 1. Pergamon Press, Oxford

Ley P 1982 Chapter 14 in: Eiser J R (ed) Social psychology and behavioral medicine. Wiley, Chichester

Livingston W 1943 Pain mechanisms. MacMillan, New York

McGhie A, Chapman J 1961 Disorders of attention and perception in early schizophrenia. British Journal of Medical Psychology 34: 103–116

McNeil B, Pauker S, Sox H, Tversky A 1982 On the elicitation of preferences for alternative therapies. New England Journal of Medicine 306: 1259–1262

McWhinney X 1972 Problem solving and decision making (The Albert Wander Lecture). Proceedings of the Royal Society of Medicine 65: initial page

Manuck S B, Harvey A H, Lechleiter S L, Neal K S 1978 Effects of coping on blood pressure responses to threat of aversive stimulation. Psychophysiology 15: 544–549

Marks I 1969 Fears and phobias. Heinemann Medical, London

Melzack R, Wall P 1965 Pain mechanisms: a new theory. Science 150: 971–979

Melzack R, Wall P 1982 The challenge of pain. Penguin Books, Harmondsworth

Nuckolls C B, Cassel J, Kaplan A H 1972 Psychosocial assets, life crises and the prognosis of pregnancy. American Journal of Epidemiology 95: 531–541

Patel C H, North W R S 1975 Randomised controlled trial of Yoga and biofeedback in management of hypertension. Lancet ii: 93–99

Paul G 1966 Insight versus desensitization in psychotherapy. Stanford University Press, Stanford

Porter A 1969 Drug defaulting in general practice. British Medical Journal 1: 218–222

Rasmussen T, Milner B 1975 Clinical and surgical studies of the cerebral speech areas in man. In: Zülch K J, Creutzfeldt O, Galbraith G C (eds) Cerebral localization. Springer-Verlag, Heidelberg

Raven J C 1948 The comparative assessment of intellectual ability. British Journal of Psychology 39: 12–19

Rees W D, Lutkins S G 1967 Mortality of bereavement. British Medical Journal 4: 13–16

Reynolds M 1978 No news in bad news: patients' views about communication in hospital. British Medical Journal 1: 1673–1676

Richman N, Stevenson J, Graham P 1982 Pre-school to school: a behavioural study. Academic press, London

Rolls E T 1975 The brain and reward. Pergamon Press

Rosenzweig M R, Bennett E L, Diamond M C 1972 Brain changes in response to experience. Scientific American 226 (February): 22–29

Schulte W, Neus H, Rüddel H 1981 Zum blutdruckverhalten Stress bei Normotonikern mit familiärer Hypertonieanamnese. Medizinische Welt 32: 1135–1137

Skilbeck C, Tulips J, Ley P 1977 The effects of fear arousal, fear perception, fear exposure and sidedness on compliance with dietary instructions. European Journal of Social Psychology 7: 221–239

Sklar L S, Anisman H 1979 Stress and coping factors influence tumor growth. Science 205: 513–515

Sloane R, Staples F, Cristol A, Yorkston N, Whipple K 1975 Psychotherapy versus behavior therapy. Harvard University Press, Cambridge

Steptoe A 1981 Psychological factors in cardiovascular disorders. Academic Press, London

Thayer B A, Papsdorf J D, Davis R, Vallecorsa S 1984 Autonomic correlates of the subjective anxiety scale. Journal of Behavioral Therapy and Experimental Psychiatry 15: 3–7

Thomas A, Chess S, Birch H G 1970 The origin of personality. Scientific American 223 (August): 102–109

Warrington, E K, Weiskrantz L 1968 A new method of testing long-term retention with special reference to amnesic patients. Nature 217: 972–974

Weiss J M 1970 Somatic effects of predictable and unpredictable shock. Psychosomatic Medicine 32: 397–408

Wolpe J 1958 Psychotherapy by reciprocal inhibition. Stanford University Press, Stanford

Index